W9-ASY-581

Sex

Other Books of Related Interest

Sex

Tamara L. Roleff, *Book Editor*

David Bender, *Publisher*
Bruno Leone, *Executive Editor*
Bonnie Szumski, *Editorial Director*
Stuart B. Miller, *Managing Editor*
James D. Torr, *Series Editor*

Teen

Decisions

Greenhaven Press Inc., San Diego, California

Library of Congress Cataloging-in-Publication Data

Sex / Tamara L. Roleff, book editor.
    p. cm. — (Teen decisions)
    Includes bibliographical references and index.
    ISBN 0-7377-0493-4 (pbk. : alk. paper) —
    ISBN 0-7377-0494-2 (lib. bdg. : alk. paper)
    1. Teenagers—Sexual behavior. 2. Sexual ethics. I. Roleff,
Tamara L., 1959–   . II. Series.

HQ27 .S458 2001
306.7'0835—dc21   00-034128
                                                                        CIP

©2001 by Greenhaven Press, Inc.
PO Box 289009, San Diego, CA 92198-9009

Printed in the U.S.A.

Contents

Foreword

The teen years are a time of transition from childhood to adulthood. By age 13, most teenagers have started the process of physical growth and sexual maturation that enables them to produce children of their own. In the United States and other industrialized nations, teens who have entered or completed puberty are still children in the eyes of the law. They remain the responsibility of their parents or guardians and are not expected to make major decisions themselves. In most of the United States, eighteen is the age of legal adulthood. However, in some states, the age of majority is nineteen, and some legal restrictions on adult activities, such as drinking alcohol, extend until age twenty-one.

This prolonged period between the onset of puberty and the achieving of legal adulthood is not just a matter of hormonal and physical change, but a learning process as well. Teens must learn to cope with influences outside the immediate family. For many teens, friends or peer groups become the basis for many of their opinions and actions. In addition, teens are influenced by TV shows, advertising, and music.

The *Teen Decisions* series aims at helping teens make responsible choices. Each book provides readers with thought-provoking advice and information from a variety of perspectives. Most of the articles in these anthologies were originally written for, and in many cases by, teens. Some of the essays focus on ethical and moral dilemmas, while others present pertinent legal and scientific information. Many of the articles tell personal stories about decisions teens have made and how their lives were affected.

One special feature of this series is the "Points of Contention," in which specially paired articles present directly opposing views on controversial topics. Additional features in each book include a listing of organizations to contact for more information, as well as a bibliography to aid readers interested in more information. The *Teen Decisions* series strives to include both trustworthy information and multiple opinions on topics important to teens, while respecting the role teens play in making their own choices.

Introduction

The teen years are a difficult time. With the onset of adolescence and puberty, teen bodies, attitudes, and feelings begin to change. Many teens—and their parents—are confused and uncertain about their developing bodies. Emerging hormones tempt many teens to explore their sexuality. Most parents want their teenagers to abstain from sexual activity until marriage or adulthood, and many are uneasy with the thought of their children becoming sexually active. At the close of the twentieth century, parents' concerns range from whether teens are emotionally mature enough to handle sex to fears of pregnancy and sexually transmitted diseases, especially HIV/AIDS. On the other hand, teens are as curious about sex as they have ever been. While some of the specific concerns about teen sex have changed over the years, a historical view of teen sex can provide valuable insight into why modern society views teen sex with alarm.

Teen Sex Versus Premarital Sex

The ages at which teens first have sex haven't changed much over the course of American history. During the 1990s, about 80 to 90 percent of teens had sexual intercourse by the time they were 20 years old; most teens were between the ages of 15 and 18 when they lost their virginity. In the 1950s the average age was 17½, according to Robert T. Michael, John H. Gagnon, Edward O. Laumann, and Gina Kolata, authors of *Sex in America: A Definitive Survey*. In the 1930s, they cite the average age as 18. And the pregnancy rate for teenage girls under 15 has barely changed during the twentieth century—approximately 12,000 girls under 15 become pregnant every year.

11

Some aspects of teen sex have changed, of course. For example, during the colonial era, poor diet delayed the arrival of puberty until 15 or 16, whereas today it's no longer uncommon for pre-teens—age 11 or 12—to undergo puberty.

More importantly, what has changed during the past two hundred years is the average age at which people marry. After the American Revolution, the states established their own legal age limits for marriage based on British common law. Although the marriage age varied from state to state, most states required girls to be 12 and boys to be 14 in order to marry (even though records show that very few children of this age were married). At the same time, the age of consent was 7. (Fears by male legislators that raising the age of consent would encourage girls to blackmail men kept the age of consent low. It wasn't until the early 1900s that most states raised the age of consent to 14.) While these ages are now considered quite young, that wasn't the view during Revolutionary times. Children were often apprenticed to learn a trade at age 6 or 7 and by the time they were in their mid- to late teens, they were earning their living.

In colonial times, then, "teen" sex was accepted as long as the teens were married. However, society closely monitored *premarital* sex. Prevailing religious beliefs considered premarital sex to be a sin, and society was also more concerned about illegitimate births. According to Kristin Luker, author of *Dubious Conceptions: The Politics of Teenage Pregnancy*, colonial communities were obligated to provide food and shelter for children who had lost a parent; providing economic aid to children of mothers who were voluntarily single was a burden that many small, rural towns couldn't support. Unmarried parents were punished for having a child out of wedlock (public whippings and fines were the common punishments). However, since unwed mothers were more visible and less able to pay fines than the fathers, women bore the brunt of the whippings. Much like Hesther Prynne in *The Scarlet Letter* was exhorted to name the father of her illegitimate child, pregnant and unwed mothers in the colonial era were commanded to name their lovers, who would then be forced to support their family.

Changing Views of Adolescence

With the advent of the Industrial Revolution, societal views of childhood and adolescence began to change. Many states passed child labor laws in the mid-1800s, which (depending on the state) prevented children under the age of 10, 12, or 14 from working. Since the children couldn't work, more children were able to attend school and communities began building more public schools. It was during this period, when children didn't have to take on the responsibilities of adulthood and they had the opportunity to play, that childhood and adolescence came to be seen as a time of innocence. Teenagers, especially girls, were viewed as vulnerable and in need of protection from the stresses of adult life. According to Luker, social reformers believed that adolescents now needed their teen years to be free of cares and worries in order to develop properly; "'burdening' them with adult concerns such as work, marriage, and sex—especially the latter two" would hinder their development into adulthood, she writes. Consequently, to protect their development, the legal age of marriage was raised to 16 for women and 18 for men.

At the same time, American psychologist G. Stanley Hall became one of the first to propose that the teenage years were a distinct stage of development between childhood and adulthood. He named this period "adolescence" in his 1904 book, *Adolescence: Its Psychology and Its Relations to Physiology, Anthropology, Sociology, Sex, Crime, Religion, and Education.* Hall writes, "The dawn of puberty is soon followed by a stormy period . . . where there is a peculiar proneness to be either very good or very bad." Hall, and many others in the early 1900s, argued that teenagers—who just one hundred years earlier were considered mature enough to work, marry, have sex, and raise children—weren't legally or emotionally developed enough to take on any adult responsibilities.

This way of thinking continued into the mid- to late twentieth century. As the legal age for marriage rose, so, too, did the average age of marriage. However, the age at which teenagers began having sex remained unchanged. Whereas the eighteen- and nineteen-year-olds who were having sex in the 1700s, 1800s, and the first half of the 1900s were usually married, many teenagers in the second half of the 1900s were having illicit sex. Robert T. Michael and his associates note in *Sex in America* that in the 1990s, the average age for marriage was in the mid-twenties. Thus, teenagers and young adults are now expected to ignore their hormones and remain chaste for a longer period than their ancestors ever did. However, many teens follow the example set by their ancestors when they were teenagers hundreds of years earlier: They give in to their urges.

The Sexual Revolution

Up until about the 1960s, society, parents, and political and religious leaders were fairly consistent about the message they gave teens about sex: Wait until marriage. Before this time, sex generally wasn't discussed or portrayed as openly as it is now. Sex education was provided by the parents, who were often too embarrassed to offer any information beyond a brief explanation of the basics. However, the message from society was very firm: "Nice" girls didn't have sex. A double standard was solidly in place: Boys were expected to have sex with as many girls as they could, while girls who were sexually active received a bad reputation. Girls (and adult women) who became pregnant often felt they must leave town so that no one would know their scandalous secret. The media also contributed to this image of innocence. Married couples on television and in the movies slept in twin beds, and girls and women who had illicit sex were usually punished somehow at the end of the script. As a result of the taboo nature of the subject, many teens married without a firm understanding of the mechanics and pleasures of sexual intercourse, and birth control—in the form of condoms—wasn't easily available to unmarried teens.

In the 1960s and early 1970s, Americans' views of sexuality and premarital sex underwent a dramatic change in a phenomenon known as the sexual revolution. Perhaps the most important event of the sexual revolution was the introduction of the birth control pill; now, for the first time, women could control their fertility. The U.S. Supreme Court also played a pivotal role in the development of the sexual revolution. In 1970 it ruled that states couldn't prohibit married couples from obtaining contraceptives, and in 1972, it legalized abortion. The women's rights movement also became a prominent social force in the 1960s, changing the way both men and women thought about gender roles. Together, these changes contributed to a powerful revolution. The easy availability of the pill and abortion allowed girls and women to have sex with little fear of pregnancy. The sexual revolution also destigmatized unwed motherhood for those girls and women who decided to keep and raise their babies. The change in how Americans viewed premarital sex is staggering; according to a Roper poll in 1969, nearly 80 percent of Americans believed that premarital sex was wrong. Four years later, that percentage dropped to 50 percent.

The Media and Sex

The media began to reflect this new, open attitude toward sex by portraying more sexual situations and language. Today, sex is the featured topic of talk shows, soap operas, and dramatic and sitcom television shows. Talk show hosts such as Jerry Springer feature sexual topics that become more and more outrageous in a bid to attract viewers. Studios use explicit heterosexual and homosexual love scenes, as well as rape, bondage, and sado-masochistic sex to draw attention to their movies and shows. Big name stars are more willing to be nude in their films. Movie and TV characters, whether friends or strangers, fall into bed and have sex with little or no discussion of contraception, pregnancy, STDs or AIDS. But Hollywood isn't the only party guilty of using sex to draw attention to its products. Music lyrics are just as explicit in words as film is in pictures. Madison Avenue produces slick ads using sex appeal to promote its products. Commercials for Victoria's Secret feature close-ups of female breasts to sell its bras; breweries use scantily-clad women to entice viewers to buy their brands of beer.

Whether parents like it or not, these continual messages and images influence teens' ideas about sex. Michael J. Basso, author of *The Underground Guide to Teenage Sexuality*, argues that teens are absorbing media messages such as:

> Sex is good. The more sexually experienced you are, the more accepted you will be. The cool guys are studs. Promiscuity is in. Fun and popular girls have sex. Girls want to have sex, even when they say no. Sex is an all-night fantasy filled with simultaneous, earth-shattering, multiple orgasms. Only the physically beautiful people really enjoy life. You don't need birth control or condoms because only other people get pregnant, STDs, or AIDS. Sex makes you a respected adult.

Peer Pressure

Teens aren't only pressured by media images to have sex, they also face pressures from their friends and peers. Teens may feel left out when they hear others talking about "doing it," "going all the way," "scoring," and "getting lucky." Boyfriends or girlfriends may pressure their partner into having sex by saying "If you loved me, you would" or other lines designed to instill feelings of guilt for not giving in. Some teens may be embarrassed to admit that they still are a virgin, and so they have sex at the first opportunity. Other teens are simply curious about the experience. Julia Anderson, a teenager in Detroit, talks about the conflicting messages teens receive about sex:

In our culture we're taught that sex is evil but you're supposed to have as much of it as possible. We're living in this huge double standard and it's really frustrating because you hear different things: Your parents tell you "Don't do it," the church tells you, "Don't do it," but your friends say, "Do it, do it, do it." TV says do it and it's in every conversation you have even if it comes up in a little inside joke or a little metaphor or something, it's in everything. I can totally understand how people just give in and say, "Fine, I want to be let in on the big, huge secret."

Parental Messages About Sex

Teens do receive a lot of conflicting messages about sex. Parents try their best to raise their children to become healthy sexual beings, but many times their advice runs contrary to teens' own hormones and the messages broadcast by the rest of society. With the benefit of age and experience, many parents know that teen sex isn't always a wise, healthy, or positive experience. Parental involvement in their children's sex education is critical to the health and well-being of their teenagers. Teens need to know what their parents' values and morals are and the possible consequences of sexual activity before they find themselves in a position where they are confronted with having to make a decision about sex.

However, parental attempts to dissuade their children from teen sex aren't always successful, and often send mixed messages. For example, parents may follow their religion's teaching that sex should be reserved for the sanctity of marriage, but if the parents weren't virgins at their wedding, it may be difficult for them to explain why they could have sex outside of marriage and why their children shouldn't. Parents may also tell a teen, "Wait until you're old enough" without making it clear when they believe their child is "old enough" to have sex. According to Basso in *The Underground Guide to Teenage Sexuality*, telling a teen that "you'll know when the right time is" or "when you meet someone special and fall in love" doesn't answer the question. Since even adults have trouble deciding when the time is right, teens are bound to feel that an answer of "You'll know" is unsatisfactory. Furthermore, Basso notes that it's also difficult trying to explain what love is:

> Teens fall in and out of love frequently. Does this mean that when young people are in love, sex is a way of expressing true love? A parent might come back with "That's just puppy love or infatuation." So what is the difference between love and infatuation? Guess what—you lose! Sure you can find all kinds of people who might be able to come up with a few goodies yourself, but when you are in love or infatuated, you experience the same emotions. Both bring very strong and very real feelings of passion.

Parents know that sex is a wonderful expression of love, but sometimes it's not easy for them to explain its complexities and prepare teenagers for its intensity and consequences.

Consequences

Nevertheless, parental guidance is crucial in the areas of teen sex. Many teens who rely on the media and their friends for their information about sex are often ignorant about the possible consequences of sexual activity. In the case of sex, ignorance can be deadly and can change a teen's life forever.

The most obvious consequences of having sex are the possibilities of becoming pregnant or contracting a sexually transmitted disease. While pregnancy and most STDs can be prevented through contraception, many teens who do have sex don't use contraception. This may be because teens receive conflicting messages about sex and contraception from the media, their peers, their parents, and their sex education classes. Teens are often told that "everyone" is having sex, and therefore, they must have sex to be a part of the "in" crowd. However, media images of sexual intercourse rarely portray the couple stopping to put on a condom. Finally, parents and religious leaders urge teens to abstain from sex. So, to appease their conscience and their parents, teens often try to prevent giving the appearance that they are ready for sex. For many teens, especially girls, this means they avoid using contraception. Luker explains the paradox in *Dubious Conceptions*:

> One simple way of showing that one is a "nice girl" is to be unprepared for sex—to have given no prior thought to contraception. . . . A woman who obtains contraception in anticipation of sexual activity is thought to be "looking for sex" (as teens say) and is culturally devalued. More to the point, she risks being devalued within the relationship. When it comes to contraception, she is caught in a net of double binds. She is the one who is supposed to "take care of it," the one at whom most contraceptive programs are aimed, and the one for whose body the most effective methods have been developed. Yet she is expected to be diffident about sex, and interested in it only because love and erotic arousal have spontaneously led her to be "carried away."

This reluctance to be prepared for sex explains why many girls say they didn't intend to become pregnant, "it just happened." And it also is partly responsible for the soaring rate of STDs— estimated at 25 percent—among sexually active teenagers.

Other, less obvious consequences of teen sex are more emotional than physical. Teens—again, mostly girls—face being labeled with a bad reputation if they appear too eager or too ready to have sex. Others may regret the circumstances surrounding the time when they lost their virginity or had sex with someone for the first time. Yet others who think they are ready for sex may be surprised at and unprepared for the feelings of loss, regret, or guilt they may experience after sex.

These consequences—pregnancy, STDs, and emotional unpreparedness—are often at the heart of debates over what types of sex education teenagers should be taught. Some parents believe that teens are going to be sexually active no matter what they are told; therefore, they argue, teens should be taught how to protect themselves from pregnancy and STDs by using contraception and other methods of "safe sex." Other adults claim, however, that telling teens about "safe sex" gives them the implied—and wrong—message that teen sex is acceptable behavior. Thus they believe that teens should receive "abstinence-only" sex education, a program that teaches teens how to say no to sex and therefore avoid the emotional and physical consequences of having sex at too young an age.

A Difficult Decision

All of these factors—the later age at which teens marry, the pervasiveness of sex in the media, and the conflicting views about sex that teens receive from their parents, peers, and society—make choices about sex some of the most difficult decisions that teens must make. And because the decision to have sex can have serious and potentially life-altering consequences for teens, it's not one that should be taken lightly. The essays in *Teen Decisions: Sex* are meant to help you identify and understand the aspects involved in making this important decision. In Chapter One, **Common Concerns About Sex**, teen advisers answer some of the questions teens might ask about their own sexuality, such as when is a teen ready to have sex? Is masturbation normal? What is sex like? In Chapter Two, **Thinking About Virginity**, teens discuss why they decided to remain a virgin and their feelings about their first sexual experience. Chapter Three, **The Pressures Teens Face to Have Sex**, examines not only peer pressure on boys and girls, but also the pressure women face from society to have sex. Sexually transmitted diseases and pregnancy are some of the topics discussed in the fourth chapter, **Sex and Consequences**. The authors in the following chapters provide advice about these subjects and try to help you understand the issues involved and to make wise and responsible choices concerning sexual activity.

Chapter 1

Common Concerns
About Sex

Only Thirteen

Teen Advice Online

Today, even thirteen-year-old girls are making decisions about having sex. However, when you decide to lose your virginity, you should think about aspects besides the physical act. Below, teen counselors advise a teenage girl that she needs to consider the emotional aspects of sex as well as the risks she faces by deciding to have sex at such an early age. The authors are peer counselors with Teen Advice Online, a teen counseling website (www.teenadviceonline.org).

I am always so horny. I have done some pretty stupid things. Like I agreed to let a 19—almost 20-year-old—go down on me. Anywayz . . . I have met this guy who's 14 and he's really sweet and funny, and adorable and HOT and like. . . . we might go out. But . . . he's not a virgin. And I am. And I'm afraid if I start fooling around with him and he wants to have sex I won't be able to say no. I mean, just hearing him talk I wanna have sex with him. But I'm also afraid I would do it wrong or that like it would hurt to much and. . . .

I think I'm ready for sex . . . but it makes me feel bad that I'm only 13. Yet I feel ready. What should I do?

Female 13 yrs.
USA

Reprinted with permission from "Being Horny Means 'Ready for Sex?'" *Teen Advice Online*, 1998. Article available at www.teenadviceonline.org/archive/19984.html.

Answers

Being physically ready and emotionally ready are two very different things. Most people can say they are physically ready for sex. I would even venture to say that. However, I know that, not only is it meant to be more of an emotional thing, there are SO many consequences to consider. Especially for you, since the guy you like is not a virgin. Having sex with someone who has had sex with other people is, essentially, like having sex with all of their other partners, and their partner's partners!! Do you see what I mean? If you know it would be hard for you to control, then I suggest making this known to this guy, or refraining from seeing him. There are too many consequences that can happen from 5 seconds of pleasure :-). Good Luck. ~Peace~

> "I think I'm ready for sex . . . but it makes me feel bad that I'm only 13."

Amanda

Consider the Consequences

Well you can have sex if you want to, but do consider the consequences—you could get pregnant, acquire an STD, have complications—did you know the sooner you have sex the greater the chances of getting cancer of the cervix, etc? There are many risks to consider when having sex, especially making sure it's the right guy and the right time.

You should wait to make sure the relationship will last, just because you're horny doesn't mean you're ready—it just means your hormones are in overdrive—it's okay to fool around but don't sacrifice your virginity to "the fool"—you may take it for granted now, but when you meet THE GUY, the one you plan to spend your life with, it will be worth the wait. If you plunge into the lusty behavior you may regret it so much later. Bad reputations are about as hard to unspread as butter.

Tina

Plenty of Time

Raging hormones are pretty much the bane of every teenager's existence. You hit puberty, and all of a sudden those hormones are going crazy. Unfortunately, a lot of teens mistake these sexual feelings to be an indication that they're ready to have sex. In reality, there's a whole lot more to being ready to become sexually active than just feeling "horny."

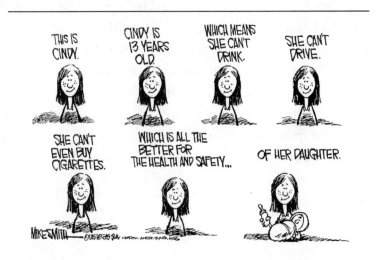

Mike Smith. Reprinted by permission of United Feature Syndicate, Inc.

First off, you have to know the risks and consequences, and be prepared for those. Having sex can lead to unwanted, unplanned pregnancy, contraction of sexually transmitted diseases, and a lot of emotional baggage. Could you handle it if you got pregnant? Do you know how to protect yourself from such a possibility? Do you know that no manner of protection works 100% of the time? What about STDs? Do you know how to protect yourself from those? Again, do you know that no manner of protection works 100% of the time? Do you know that some STDs are deadly and/or incurable? Sex is a big responsibility, and you have to be sure that you can handle that responsibility before you even think about taking it on.

You're young, only thirteen years old. You have plenty of time to become sexually active. It's a big decision, so just take your time and don't rush into anything. Before you have sex for the first time, you should know beyond a shadow of a doubt that this is what you want, that you're 100% ready to handle it and be responsible about it. If you can, talk to people you trust about this decision you're trying to make—your friends and family. They might have some valuable advice for you. I hope this helps. Best of luck to you.

Love, Jen

Barely a Teenager

I'm not going to lecture you that you're too young for sex. If you really want to do it you're going to whether I tell you to or not, but I would like you [to] step out for a second and look at yourself.

You're 13—barely a teenager. Do a lot of the 13-year-olds you know have sex lives? I doubt it. Sex is something mature people do and at that age you're still developing. Throwing sex into your life (as good as it may feel) isn't always the best choice.

You're at an age where your hormones are going to tell you to do a lot of things, but this is a time when you really should be listening to your mind. I can tell you're a smart person because you admit that you have second doubts about it. You're not sleeping around with a bunch of guys simply because it "feels good." You've gotta be smart about this. Do you want to get pregnant or AIDS before you're 14? Do you think a 14-year-old guy is old enough to be a responsible sexual partner? Or are you so hypnotized by his voice and body that you'd be willing to throw caution in the wind in exchange for an hour or two of hot sex?

I can't tell you what to do, but it would be a shame for you to write back in a year or so asking me about a pregnancy or a sexually-transmitted disease.

You're a smart girl and I trust you'll make the right decision. Take care,

Laura

Masturbation Is Healthy

Liberated Christians, Inc.

Although a lot of myths still surround masturbation, over the years societal and medical views of masturbation have changed from considering it a sin to viewing it as a means of sexual and emotional release. According to this author, masturbation is a natural, healthy, and risk-free way to experience sexual pleasure. In fact, sex researchers believe that regular masturbation keeps you healthy mentally and physically. Finally, it can help you learn what sexual activities you enjoy the most; this knowledge, when passed along to your partner, can enhance your sexual pleasure. Liberated Christians, Inc., is a couples fellowship group that promotes sexual intimacy in alternative, nonmonogamous relationships.

You are not insane. You are not blind. You have not grown hair on your palms. You are a completely competent member of society—despite all the times you've done it. Kinsey and the latest *Sex in America* report show there's a whole lot of shaking going on. Today's sex researchers have come to grips with the fact that masturbation has important physical and emotional benefits for both men and women.

Getting a Grip

"Masturbation is a normal, natural activity throughout life," says Robert Pollack, a psychology professor at the University of Georgia. It may even contribute to mental health and not doing it may lead to psychosexual problems.

For men, masturbation or regular sex is good for the prostate and can prevent painful prostate blockage. For women it can help reduce cramping and for both men and women has been shown to have a healthy effect on the immune systems as well as reducing overall tension and helping emotions.

Besides being healthy for the body, a private grope can help both a man and a woman better understand their own sexuality. If you can learn to lie back and enjoy it and really pay attention to the pleasure it gives your body—no one knows better than you what gives you maximum pleasure—you can share that knowledge with a partner and have more mutually fulfilling sexual pleasure sharing. The self-awareness gained from masturbation makes it a central feature of many sex therapy programs.

An Evolutionary Design

Evolution may have even designed us to be masturbators. Notice when you are standing where your hand falls if you hang it in front of you. Apes do it, dogs and cats do it, elephants do it and even porcupines have been observed doing it, probably very carefully. One reason we may be so programmed, paradoxically, is to increase our odds of producing offspring. Older sperm can lose their ability to swim well. A good masturbatory flush guarantees fresh, robust sperm for mating.

> [Masturbation] may even contribute to mental health and not doing it may lead to psychosexual problems.

Storing seminal fluids for long periods can also cause prostate congestion, which in turn can lead to urinary and ejaculatory pain. Regular ejaculations, either through masturbation or intercourse, can help ward off this condition, also called non-specific prostatitis and, for obvious reasons, "sailor's disease" and "priest's disease."

Masturbation is also an ever-renewable health resource. In fact, the people who start the earliest and do it the most often are the ones who do it longest into old age. So, as with all sexual activity, it's "use it or lose it."

Normal and Common

Some things you need to know about masturbation:

• It's normal. Two-thirds of men and women questioned for the 1993 Janus Report on Sexual Behavior agreed with the statement that "Masturbation is a natural part of life and continues on in marriage"; 48 percent of the single men and 68 percent of the divorced men reported doing it daily to weekly. And in a 1995 international survey, *Playboy* found that at least 15 percent of its American readers masturbated daily.

• It's a mark of intelligence. Maybe. *Sex in America*, the 1994 University of Chicago study, linked the practice to education: Eighty percent of men with graduate degrees reported masturbating in the current year, as opposed to less than 50 percent of the high-school dropouts.

• Even married guys do it. It isn't limited to the romantically challenged. According to the Janus report, 44 percent of married men masturbate once a week or more.

Stephen Rae, *Men's Health*, September 1995.

Another reason why nature designed us to masturbate is to strengthen PC muscles, much like "Kegel" exercises. This is especially true in females where strong PC muscles are practically the sole factor in whether labor is easy and fast or long and difficult. Females masturbating regularly with multiple orgasms would develop strong PC muscles and should have easier labor.

Another potential concern is reliance on masturbation for sexual pleasure to the exclusion of intimacy with another person. But in such cases, masturbation is probably a symptom, not a cause, of larger psychological barriers to intimacy. Most people want relationships. But if you're scared of them, you might stick with masturbation exclusively.

How Masturbation Got Its Bad Rap

First came the misunderstanding of the biblical passage related to Onan whose sin was not masturbation but not impregnating his dead brother's wife. Then came the twisted Christian tradition that sex was only proper for procreation, not just enjoyment. The stigma was later compounded by the 18th century Swiss physician Samuel August Tissot who believed that while blood-flow changes during any kind of sex would cause nerve damage and insanity, masturbation was especially hazardous.

> Besides being healthy for the body, a private grope can help both a man and a woman better understand their own sexuality.

Tissot's teachings were picked up by American physician Benjamin Rush. Besides signing the Declaration of Independence, Rush wrote several influential articles on masturbation that helped make it one of the most feared activities in the new United States. Antimasturbatory devices became available, including a tube lined with metal spikes that fit over the penis. Until this century, young men were sometimes put to bed in straitjackets or with their hands tied to bedposts to make sure they didn't do it.

John Harvey Kellogg, of cornflakes fame, was a virulent crusader against masturbation and invented the cereal as one element of a diet he thought would quench the sex drive. (Mr. Sylvester Graham came up with the Graham cracker for the same purpose.) For those masturbators whom snacks could not cure, Kellogg suggested circumcision without anesthesia.

Finally, around the turn of the century, physicians started to realize that masturbation was not the evil earlier generations thought it was. Still, it was not until 1940 that a respected textbook, *Diseases of Infancy and Childhood,* removed its discussion of masturbation from the chapter titled "Functional and Nervous Disorders."

An internet message in reply to above post:

> Quite true. The sad preoccupation with masturbation came from Jansenism, a heresy which said the Human Body is inherently evil. . . . As a Catholic Priest, I have sorrowed greatly at the unnecessary neurosis our Catholic Church has fostered regarding masturbation. . . . Glad you have this out there.

A women said on the internet:

> Sexual release is just as important as any kind of emotional release. Saying that you shouldn't masturbate is like saying that you shouldn't cry when you're upset or hurt, or that you should hold in anger and other emotions. I see no difference between sexual release and emotional release. Not releasing will only result in stress and health problems. And I know that I need no more stress in my life. I figure, if something helps a person relieve stress, clear their mind, and make them feel better (that doesn't hurt others, mind you), then more power to them.

Ready for Sex

Joshua

In this personal narrative of his first sexual experience, Joshua writes about the hopes and expectations he had for his first time. He writes about how he turned down an opportunity to have sex with his girlfriend because of the pressure and awkwardness of the moment. However, when he and his girlfriend eventually did have sex, it happened during a moment of spontaneous passion that he doesn't regret. Joshua is a teenager who writes for *Teenwire,* a Planned Parenthood online magazine.

M om and Dad's idea of sex education: If you're gonna have sex with someone, you'd better make sure you love them. Cause if you don't, you're gonna roll over the next morning and hate them. This idea did wonders for keeping me a virgin.

Julie was my best friend's girlfriend. I was their counselor, their go-between. She'd call me to complain, I'd call him to explain, they'd get together and make up while I sat around and wondered what it would be like to be in their shoes.

They broke up for good a couple of months later. Junior year. She wore red velvet sunglasses. I fell in love with her. Sweet Julie . . .

When you fall in love with a friend it's easy to create an ideal present and fantasy future. We were together for a couple of years. I'd have Christmas brunch at her grandmother's. She'd play board games and dance with my folks on Christmas night. Once we stayed up late making a list of baby names. When she got her first car, we'd drive around and choose houses. She gave me a bowl of cherries on the Fourth of July.

> "I don't know if other couples talk about it . . . , but I wanted it to be natural and spontaneous."

Her parents were pretty cool about us hanging out in her room. Yeah, we fooled around a bit. Fingers flying and bodies rubbing, but never going all the way. I don't know if other couples talk about it ("When do you wanna do it? Tonight? Next Saturday? After six months?"), but I wanted it to be natural and spontaneous.

If Not Tonight, When?

Senior Prom came. Her dad rented us a limo and we had dinner at the Ritz-Carlton. The night was romantic but contrived. After dinner, the limo took us to the beach for a long walk and a little illegal champagne. We dropped by the prom for a couple of dances and some pictures, then she surprised me—her friend's parents had a condo on the beach.

The mood changed as soon as we walked into the condo—all this pressure swooped down on us. There we were alone in this condo, and not to watch TV or kick back to music. We were there for sex. It wasn't right. It was like a movie set, and we were the actors, ready to start "hittin' it" on cue. I knew there were probably a lot of couples hittin' it on prom night, but I'm not about playing the part. I dare to be different. We didn't do it. She wasn't happy.

The rest of the night was awkward. A bunch of our friends had rented hotel suites. We joined them for an all-night party chasing each other with fire extinguishers, smoking cigars, and yes, some were having sex.

But though the night was awkward, it was also cool. Watching our friends head off to have sex kind of disgusted Julie—all of a sudden it's like we were the adults, and our friends were these kids stupidly humping away their virginity on a drunken prom night. I was off the hook.

When the Time Is Right

A couple of weeks later I was hanging out at my buddy's house while his parents were out of town. It was about two in the afternoon, hot and humid. It was the kind of day you don't expect much from, just the chance to chill with your friends. Julie came over. When she arrived, the air was electric. The heat gave her a thin film of sweat, she was slightly out of breath, and she smelled like summer. We kissed like it was the first time, and quickly fell into bed. "This is it," I'm thinking.

Every conversation I'd ever had about sex, every image of sex I'd ever seen came flooding through my mind. I was completely obsessed with how I was doing, and whether this would be memorable. I'm not going to admit I was nervous. It's weird how we were naked, getting all private, but we never asked each other out loud what we wanted each other to do next. She did ask me if I had a condom. I did (the old wallet standby, which thankfully didn't break).

> "I was completely obsessed with how I was doing, and whether this would be memorable."

I opened it up and she put it on, and . . . it was a beautiful day.

Looking back I'm pretty cool with having waited until the end of high school to have sex. Right after we all graduated I went to a party and a bunch of guys were talking about virginity. It's like we all thought each other got laid for the first time at 15 or 16. But just about all of us were virgins until senior year or after. Figures.

Not Ready for Sex

DeDe Lahman

Many teens consider losing their virginity as a rite of passage, an act that turns them into men or women. Some teens are so anxious for this transformation that they'll have sex with someone at the first opportunity, a decision that they often later regret. DeDe Lahman describes how she felt as her close girlfriends lost their virginity, and discusses her own feelings about her virginity. She decides that she really doesn't like or trust any boy well enough to have sex with him, a sign that she takes to mean that she's not ready for sex. She's proud of her decision to wait, and realizes that sex isn't something that you lose or give away. Lahman writes for *Seventeen* magazine.

I never actually planned on being a virgin all through high school. I mean, it's not like I wasn't interested in sex. In fact, I thought about it all the time, envisioning my first experience to be very romantic—a fun evening, a warm, safe place, a guy I really loved and trusted and cared about a lot. I think that's what most people hope for. But when I hit high school, everyone else seemed to, like, forget that vision and replace it with a different attitude: Just do it.

There were only 205 kids in my class at a New England prep

Reprinted from "Sex Appeal," by DeDe Lahman, *Seventeen,* March 1997. Reprinted with permission from Primedia Publications.

school (if someone even tripped in the lunchroom, everyone else knew about it by next period). Freshman year, my four closest girlfriends and I all started out in the same place sexually: Most of us had made out with a few guys, and some of us had even gotten to second base (at least over the shirt, if not under the bra).

But then we were invited to the first upperclass party of the year, and everything changed.

The Party

It was thrown by Veronica Leeds,* the coolest senior in school. Veronica had brown hair with chunky blond streaks and wore black lipstick. Every guy worshiped her. When we arrived at the party, my friends and I tried to play it cool, babbling to each other nervously but not actually saying anything coherent except "Oh, my God, [*fill in the name of someone hot*] is here." I felt way out of my league and spent most of the night maneuvering through the sweaty, crowded rooms, stepping over clusters of bodies, trying not to stare while people danced and hooked up and seriously partied.

Though my friends and I stayed in our group, a couple of senior guys flirted with us—a minitriumph, considering the majority of girls who scoffed at us condescendingly (that was just how you treated frosh girls at my school). Then, around the time of my curfew, I watched my friend Samantha slip through the back screen door with A.J.—one of the guys we had been talking to (who was also rumored to be one of the biggest players in school). She grinned back at the rest of us and mouthed, "Leave without me."

> I never actually planned on being a virgin all through high school.

At our lockers Monday morning, we all crowded expectantly around Samantha, who acted way too nonchalant about the

---

*All names have been changed.

whole thing and dodged our probing questions like a skilled politician. But by the very end of first period, she had turned into somewhat of a celebrity, which made it hard for her to blow it off. All the freshman girls had heard the rumors, and as we ushered Samantha toward the bathroom, they scanned her up and down, clutching their books tightly against their chests. It dawned on us that the whole school knew, and as we walked through the halls to our classes, guys who had never even glanced our way before were saying hi.

Empty and Cold

At noon, when Samantha and I finally reached the cafeteria alone, I pumped her for info. I was so excited to get the scoop. I mean, wow. Sex. It was such a major, adult thing. I wanted to know everything: What happened? What did he say? Did it hurt?

I held my breath, waiting for the tales of romance—the really cool story about the way he had first kissed her, what it had felt like, the deep connection they now shared. But Samantha just looked blankly at me, her eyes red-rimmed and watery.

It was no big deal, she said. Basically, they had gone outside to talk, she got very drunk on cranberry juice and vodka, and the next thing she knew, they were on the ground having sex—kind of in the bushes on the perimeter of the backyard. She didn't really remember many details and had no clue about whether he'd used a condom, but she was pretty sure he hadn't.

While she was talking, I got this weird feeling. It was as if she hadn't really been there in her body—as if what she was describing had happened to somebody else. I'd always thought that sex, especially sex for the first time, was supposed to be this huge expression of love (or at least very serious *like),* something that two people did when they really trusted and cared about each other—so getting "done" in the bushes on top of wet, smelly leaves didn't seem very loving or warm to me. Suddenly, it didn't seem like what had happened was very exciting at all. In fact, it seemed kind of empty and cold.

Later that day, we walked by A.J. in the library, and he looked right through Samantha, like she was Casper or something. Luckily, Samantha didn't end up getting pregnant or contracting an STD or anything, and a few weeks later, she started going out with a new guy. And then, one by one, almost every one of my friends lost her virginity—as if being a virgin were some trend that wasn't "in" anymore, like baby barrettes or strappy sandals.

I Wasn't Ready

As each girl went through her big post-losing-it phase (talking about it incessantly, reveling in her new "womanhood," worrying about late periods), I couldn't help but feel further and further out of the loop. It was like all of my closest friends were part of this secret club to which I didn't belong, and it started to get me down. Fortunately, my friends were cool enough not to make a big deal out of my "hymenally challenged" status: Since I wasn't questioning my decision, they weren't either. And as much as they thought they'd been ready, deep down inside I had plenty of reasons that let me know I wasn't.

> I'd always thought that sex, especially sex for the first time, was supposed to be this huge expression of love.

Like, first of all, what guy would I do it with? There wasn't anyone I was truly in love with—or even very much in like with. And even if there were, he'd have to be the type who would still talk to me and respect me and hang out with me the next day. And what if we broke up afterward—would I be able to deal? Second, I had a hard enough time being completely stark naked with *myself,* let alone parading around in front of some guy. (I couldn't even think about going to the gyno without breaking into a cold sweat.) Third, I could never imagine buying a condom, not to mention just whipping out a trusty tube of spermicidal gel in the middle of the whole event and, like, casually talking it over with my crush. Fourth, I didn't know one guy who would have sex with me and not announce it over the PA system. And fifth? I was scared of the pain—too scared to get past it and think about the rest, like how I'd be sharing myself with someone in a really major way.

Weeding Out the Jerks

All this was a clear signal that I was not ready, but what wasn't clear was how to handle the sex thing when I was with someone I liked. So what I decided to do was to be up front with the guy: After a few weeks of getting closer, I'd let him know the deal. Which you'd think might make a lot of guys walk away, but I could tell that most of them respected my honesty and appreciated that there were some boundaries (I found that not every guy automatically wanted to leap into bed, either). This became an easy way for me to weed out the jerks: If they couldn't deal with my decision, then they couldn't deal with me.

A few years ago, I read a cool passage about virginity in a psychology book. It said that the word "virgin" did not originally refer to a women who had not yet had intercourse but to a woman who was not tied to—or possessed by—any man. In other words, it meant a woman who was her own person, both sexually and socially. Reading that made me feel really good about myself and proud of my decision not to have treated virginity as this part of me I had to "lose" or "give away." I'd always known that sex is meant to be an experience that makes you—and your relationship—strong and whole and complete. And until I was sure that was how it would make me feel, why should I have settled for anything less?

The First Time

Tanya Maloney

For some teens, the decision to have sex isn't something that they plan, "it just happens." Most people hope that their first time will be like a romantic love scene in a Hollywood movie, but the reality usually does not live up to expectations. A man's first sexual experience is usually quite different than a woman's, who may not even reach orgasm. Tanya Maloney, an advice columnist for Sex Etc., a website written by and for teens, describes what sex is like for both men and women.

"**A**re you still coming to get me after school tomorrow?" Jessica asked her boyfriend, James.

"Yeah, I'll meet you out front," he said.

"All right, see you tomorrow . . ."

The First Time

And that was the only thing the couple planned. The rest just happened. James picked Jessica up from school and they went to his house. They went straight to his room, watched some music videos and started to kiss. The kiss led to so much more.

The two had been dating on and off for almost two years and often considered having sex. James suggested it first, but Jessi-

Reprinted from "Losing It: What's the First Time Really Like?" by Tanya Maloney, *Sex Etc.*, Winter 1997. Reprinted with permission from *Sex Etc.*, a national newsletter written by teens for teens of high school age, published by the Network for Family Life Education, Rutgers University School of Social Work.

ca wasn't sure it was the right thing to do. They never really came to an agreement. But that day after school, without saying it out loud, James and Jessica agreed to have sex.

"We didn't say what we were going to do. It was just something we assumed was going to happen," explains Jessica, 16, who lost her virginity that day just a couple of months ago.

Jessica agreed to talk to SEX, Etc. about her first time to dispel some of the mystery surrounding sex. Of course, everybody's first time is different. But since it's tough to make smart decisions when all those emotions and hormones are kicking around, we thought a look at what happened to two teens would help us all become better informed—and more sexually responsible.

> For most people, the first time is filled with high expectations and worries over whether you'll "perform" OK.

For most people, the first time is filled with high expectations and worries over whether you'll "perform" OK. Little communication or planning, no birth control and disappointment are also usually part of the picture, psychologist and American University professor Dr. Barry McCarthy explains in *Losing It: The Virginity Myth,* a book about first sexual experiences, edited by Louis M. Crosier. But with solid information, teens can make the right decisions about their own sexuality. That means waiting until you and your honey can rap seriously about sex, take precautions (read: use birth control and condoms) and understand how your bodies work sexually. Doing this before losing your virginity can make sex a source of pleasure, rather than guilt, confusion or shame, writes Dennis M. Dailey, a professor at the University of Kansas School of Social Welfare, in *Losing It: The Virginity Myth.*

Getting Physical

Most teens wonder what sex feels like the first time. The answer is usually different for guys and girls. Most guys have an orgasm the first time. A lot (one in four) have problems, though. Some can't get an erection, some ejaculate (come) before the penis penetrates the vagina, some just can't reach orgasm. "Young men are so anxious about doing well that the anxiety overpowers their ability to gain control," explains Dailey.

What's more, less than 5 percent of women have an orgasm the first time they have sex. Why? "Young men do not under-

---

Is Sex Really Like It Is in the Movies?

We live in a media (TV, movies, music, news) controlled society. The media repeatedly show us sex in ways that are inaccurate, unbelievable, idealistic, and often harmful to us. Media myths say that in order for the male to be a "stud," he should have a ten-inch monster penis, keep an erection for at least half an hour, and know where to touch and how to excite his partner. And of course the male must be aggressive. Media myths say that for the female to excite and stimulate her partner, she should be aggressive or the exact opposite: let herself be dominated. Also for the female to be successful, she should know where and how to touch her partner, have big breasts, moan and scream, and of course have an orgasm.

Constantly watching these media myths will soon start you thinking that this is how intercourse is supposed to be. This is not good.

Many people have problems with intercourse because of what could be called "performance anxiety." These people believe that if they do not do it "right" (as seen on TV), they will be inadequate, degraded (put down), and embarrassed.

To repeat, intercourse is not a performance or an Olympic event. Ideally it should be an extension or enhancement of love. The things that you see on TV and in the movies are faked performances for an audience.

Michael J. Basso, *The Underground Guide to Teenage Sexuality,* 1997.

---

stand very much about female sexuality (or their own for that matter) and neither do a lot of women," writes Dailey. "Thus, women cannot tell men what they want and most men do not have a clue."

Jessica confirms this. She says that sex hurt a little, almost like a pinch, but that "after awhile the pain eases up." So when the pain fades, does it feel pleasurable? Yes, says Jessica, but she never hit the point where you scream and yell for God, like in the movies. And she didn't have an orgasm.

Tim, who lost his virginity in seventh grade, had a different experience. Now 19, he says that, physically, sex was "the best feeling in the world. Only love feels better." And he did have an orgasm.

> Most teens wonder what sex feels like the first time. . . . Most guys have an orgasm the first time.

The emotional side of sex was trickier. Looking back now, Tim feels he was way young for sex. He remembers having the jitters, big time. "Don't let anyone try to tell you they weren't nervous the first time because they'll be lying," says Tim. Seeing a naked girl for the first time can overwhelm a teenage boy.

Plus, the girl expects the boy to know what he's doing, Tim says, admitting he didn't have a clue.

"All you can go by is what you see on TV and jump in bed and do it," he adds. (It's a bummer, but surveys show that many teens think that "Hollywood" sex is the way it really happens. Guess again).

"If I knew then what I know now, I wouldn't have done it so early," he says, referring to issues like pregnancy and disease. But, he adds that he and his girlfriend discussed sex before they did it, and they agreed to use a condom. Jessica didn't take those precautions and so she started worrying about pregnancy afterward. She wished that she had used a condom. She was lucky— she didn't become pregnant.

Now, Jessica says she feels closer to her boyfriend and can even positively say that she loves him. But she is reluctant to have sex with him too often. "I don't want him to think the relationship revolves around having sex," Jessica explains.

Healthy Sexuality

It's pretty safe to say that at one point or another, most people will lose their virginity. It's only natural.

"The healthy question is how and when to express sexuality," writes McCarthy. It's also important to consider the many reasons to wait to express your sexuality by having sexual intercourse with someone.

Adolescence is a time to learn about yourself. That means exploring your own values and beliefs and resisting pressure to have sex before you feel ready, says McCarthy. You might turn to books (check out your local library) or a trusted adult to learn how sex feels physically and emotionally for both guys and girls and how it affects relationships. Masturbation is also a good way to explore your own body.

"A healthy guideline is to view sexuality as a positive part of yourself and express it in a way that enhances your life and relationships," writes McCarthy. "At a minimum, this means trying to avoid behavior that is harmful to you or your partner—unwanted pregnancy, STDs, HIV/AIDS, sexual victimization and force or coercion. Hopefully, it means being a sexual friend who is aware and responsible."

Point of Contention: Are Homosexual Feelings Normal for Teens?

Attitudes toward homosexuality—in which an individual has sexual feelings for another person of the same sex—have generally not been very accepting, and many homosexuals have responded by keeping their sexual orientation a secret. Since the gay liberation movement of the 1970s, more and more gays and lesbians have "come out" about their sexual orientation. This openness doesn't necessarily mean that all of society has become more tolerant of homosexuality, however, and teens who experience homosexual feelings may receive conflicting messages. Many people believe the Bible condemns homosexuality as sinful and immoral behavior. They claim that individuals who become gay or lesbian have made a choice to do so, and that intensive counseling can convert them from homosexuality to heterosexuality. Others maintain that homosexuality is a normal part of the human condition that can't be changed. Since no one would willingly choose to be a gay or lesbian and become an outcast from society, these supporters argue, homosexuality must be genetically based. Understanding the argument over whether homosexuality is a result of environmental or genetic factors can help you decide for yourself whether homosexuality is a normal part of human sexuality. Kevin Cranston and Cooper Thompson wrote this brochure for gay youth and young men questioning their sexuality with the help of the Boston Area Gay and Lesbian Youth organization. Tim Stafford is the author of *Love, Sex, and the Whole Person: (Everything You Want to Know)*.

Yes: Homosexual Feelings Are Normal for Teens

Kevin Cranston and Cooper Thompson

What Does It Mean to Be Gay?

Men who call themselves gay are sexually attracted to and fall in love with other men. Their sexual feelings toward men are normal and natural for them. These feelings emerge when they are boys and the feelings continue into adulthood. Although some gay men may also be attracted to women, they usually say that their feelings for men are stronger and more important to them.

We know that about one out of ten people in the world is gay or lesbian (lesbians are women who are attracted to other women). This means that in any large group of people, there are usually several gay people present. However, you cannot tell if someone is gay or not unless he or she wants you to know. Gay people blend right in with other people. But they often feel different from other people.

Gay teenagers may not be able to specify just why they feel different. All of the guys they know seem to be attracted to girls, so they don't know where they fit in. And, they may not feel comfortable talking with an adult about their feelings.

How Do I Know if I'm Gay?

I don't remember exactly when I first knew I was gay, but I do remember that the thought of sex with men always excited me.—Alan, age 19.

I never had any real attraction towards women, but I really knew that I was gay when puberty began. I felt an attraction toward the other boys and I was curious to find out what they were like.—James, age 17.

One day I was flipping through a magazine, there was a cute guy, and bam! I knew.—Antonio, age 16.

You may not know what to call your sexual feelings. You don't have to rush and decide how to label yourself right now. Our sexual identities develop over time. Most adolescent boys are intensely sexual during the years around puberty (usually between 11 and 15 years old), when their bodies start changing and their hormones are flowing in new ways. Your sexual feelings may be so strong that they are not directed toward particular persons or situations, but seem to emerge without cause. As you get older you will figure out who you are really attracted to.

> We all choose to have sex in different ways, whether we are gay or straight.

Boys with truly gay feelings find that, over time, their attractions to boys and men get more and more clearly focused. You may find yourself falling in love with your classmates or maybe developing a crush on a particular adult man. You may find these experiences pleasurable, troubling, or a mix of the two. By age 16 or 17 many gay kids start thinking about what to call themselves, while others prefer to wait.

If you think you might be gay, ask yourself:
- When I dream or fantasize sexually, is it about boys or girls?
- Have I ever had a crush or been in love with a boy or a man?
- Do I feel different than other guys?

• Are my feelings for boys and men true and clear?

If you cannot answer these questions now, don't worry. You will be more sure in time. You and only you know how to label yourself correctly.

Making Contact

So, you may be ready to find out more. Start by reading. If you feel comfortable, ask the librarian in the "Young Adult" section of your public library. Librarians are usually glad to help. If your library does not have much on sexuality you may want to check out the "GAY" section of a large bookstore, or possibly order books and other material through the mail. Please note that not all books about gay people are supportive.

Try calling a gay hotline. Most major cities have one. You may want to call from a phone booth for privacy. They will let you talk about your feelings and will direct you to organizations that help gay people. There may even be a gay youth group in your area. . . .

Remember, gay people are out there, wherever you are. Trust your instincts. Sooner or later you will meet someone who feels some of the same things you do.

> When I first met another gay person, I felt excited, anxious, nervous and happy. There was an indescribable relief to know that I was not alone, that there was someone else like me. It was also intimidating, not knowing what to expect, but I quickly loosened up and felt relaxed.—Nathan, age 18.

> When I first made contact with another gay man, I felt a tremendous relief. I couldn't believe I had made a connection. I felt happy but also scared. I felt that I could do or say anything and not worry about it.—Alan, age 19.

> When I first met another gay person, it was incredible, refreshing, reassuring, touching, awesome, and wonderful.—James, age 17.

Will I Ever Have Sex?

Naturally, you think about finding an outlet for your sexual feelings. Becoming a healthy sexual person is part of the coming out process. You may be scared at the prospect of having sex. This is normal for everyone. No one should start having sex until they are ready. Until then, you may choose to masturbate or fantasize.

Sex should only happen between mature individuals who care about each other. You will know when the time is right.

We all choose to have sex in different ways, whether we are gay or straight. Gay men choose from a wide range of sexual practices, including masturbation (either alone or with another person), oral sex, anal intercourse, kissing, hugging, massage, wrestling, holding hands, cuddling or anything else that appeals to both partners. You are in complete control over what you do sexually and with whom.

What About AIDS?

All sexually active people need to be aware of AIDS as well as other sexually transmitted diseases. Being gay does not give you AIDS, but certain sexual practices and certain drug use behaviors can put you at risk for catching the virus that causes AIDS. AIDS is incurable, but is preventable.

Here's how to reduce your risk of getting AIDS:
- Do not shoot up drugs. Sharing needles is the most dangerous behavior in terms of getting AIDS.
- Avoid anal intercourse or other direct anal contact. Anal intercourse transmits the virus very efficiently. If you do engage in anal sex, use a condom every time.
- Use condoms whenever you engage in anal or oral sex (or vaginal sex if you have sex with women). You

should choose latex condoms that are fresh and undamaged. Store them away from heat (your wallet is not a good place to keep them). Use a condom only once. Try to choose condoms with "reservoir tips," and be sure to squeeze out the air from the tip as you put it on. Hold on to the condom as you remove your penis; sometimes they slip off after sex.

- Choose sexual activities that do not involve intercourse: hugging, kissing, talking, massaging, wrestling or masturbating (on unbroken skin).

Learning to Like Yourself

I had to reject a lot of negative heterosexual and religious programming that made me feel lousy about myself as a gay person. I began to like myself by meeting other gay people and going to a gay support group. After that I was content with myself.—Bill, age 18.

My aunt is a lesbian, and she made it clear to me, before I even knew I was gay, that being gay was OK.—Antonio, age 16.

I accepted the facts, which means that I don't deny being gay and I don't pretend to be someone I'm not.—Alan, age 19.

It's not easy to discover that you are gay. Our society makes it very clear what it thinks of gay people. We all hear the terrible jokes, the hurtful stereotypes and the wrong ideas that circulate about gay people. People tend to hate or fear what they don't understand. Some people hate lesbians and gay men. Many people are uncomfortable being around lesbians and gay men.

It's no wonder that you might choose to hide your gay feelings from others. You might even be tempted to hide them from yourself.

You may wonder if you are normal. Perhaps you worry

about people finding out about you. Maybe you avoid other kids who might be gay because of what people will think. Working this hard to conceal your thoughts and feelings is called being in the closet. It is a painful and lonely place to be, even if you stay there in order to survive.

It takes a lot of energy to deny your feelings, and it can be costly. You may have tried using alcohol or other drugs to numb yourself against these thoughts. You may have considered suicide. If so, please consult the phone book for the Samaritans or other hotline. There are alternatives to denying your very valuable feelings. Check out the resources listed on the back of this brochure.

Who Should I Tell?

I only tell other people that I'm gay if I've known them for a long time and if they are accepting and tolerant. I think it's important that they know about this special part of me.—Bill, age 18.

Since I'm normal, I don't have to hide how I feel. But you should make sure that you are comfortable with your preference before you blurt it out to just anyone.—Nathan, age 19.

I tell people that I'm gay if I know that they won't reject me, will accept me for what I am, and won't try to 'straighten' me out. I test them, I suppose, then I judge if I want to risk telling them.—James, age 17.

More and more gay kids are learning to feel better about themselves. As you start to listen to your deepest feelings and learn more about what it means to be gay you will begin to be comfortable with your sexuality. This is the process called coming out.

The first step in coming out is to tell yourself that you are gay and say, "That's OK." Later you may want to tell someone else—someone you trust to be understanding and sympathetic. You might choose a friend or an adult. You will probably want to meet other gay kids for friendship or a more intimate relationship. Some gay kids are able to come out to their families. You need to decide whether or not to tell your family, and to choose the right time. Lots of people, including parents, simply don't understand gay people and are difficult to come out to. In the beginning, be cautious about whom you tell.

But it is crucial to be honest with yourself. Just as self-denial costs you, coming out pays off. Most kids who accept their sexuality say they feel calmer, happier and more confident.

> No matter what people say, you are normal. God created you, and you were made in this [sic] image. If you are non-religious, you were born and you have a purpose, and being gay is only part of it.—Nathan, age 19.

> Stand up for what you believe in, and don't listen to what hatemongers have to say. Stay proud and confident.—James, age 17.

Reprinted from "I Think I Might Be Gay . . . Now What Do I Do?" by Kevin Cranston and Cooper Thompson. Reprinted with permission from The Campaign to End Homophobia.

No: Homosexual Feelings Are Not Normal

Tim Stafford

Q: I am gay. Or at least bisexual. I am also a Christian. I have been a Christian for four years. Most people's response to these facts is, "Well, if you made a true commitment, you wouldn't struggle with this." Or, "You can't be a Christian and be gay too." So I am a poor excuse for a Christian. I know what I do is wrong, but I still go on and do it. That is why I am writing to you. What's wrong with *me? Do I need psychological help? Are you going to give me the "Jesus is the true answer" bit? (Though I know he is.) I just can't do it alone. I don't even know if I want to change. What should I do?*

A: Let me start with your comment that you are a poor excuse for a Christian. There, at least, we are on common ground. I am a poor excuse for a Christian. We all are, if I read my Bible correctly. Nobody deserves to be treated lovingly by God; we all act in ways that would justify his turning away from us. Recognizing our total lack of credibility before him is a necessary starting point for grasping his attitude toward us. Because instead of turning from us, God welcomes us into his family and calls us his children.

God does not stop there, however. Any loving father trains his children, wanting them to grow up healthy. For your own good, God has expressed his expectations regarding your choices. He is not ambiguous. God does not want you living a gay lifestyle.

The Bible's Views
The Bible considers homosexual actions wrong. There isn't a great deal of material dealing with it; in the Old Testament it simply is declared off-limits, and that is carried over in the New Testament. The only passage that gives a hint of why it is wrong is Romans 1:26–27. There Paul discusses homosexuality in the context of people that have turned their back on God and have succeeded in twisting far away from what is "natural." Paul probably was thinking of the story of creation in Genesis, where it is said that God made man in his own image "male and female." We're sexual people—that's what's "natural"—and sex was made to be between male and female. We learn something about ourselves and about God through the wonderful

52

erotic attraction and interaction of male and female. We learn even if we never marry, for we take part in those interactions at other levels.

That is the basic threat—that you would lose out on part of your identity. Your true identity in Christ isn't homosexual. Some experts say nearly everyone has homosexual desires to some extent. But the sexual focus of our lives is meant to be the opposite sex, for that is how we discover more about ourselves.

The Big Lie

It is important to distinguish between your personality structure and the way you live it out. In other words, there is a difference between homosexual tendencies and a homosexual lifestyle. Everyone has certain dispositions that lead to particular strengths and weaknesses. The Big Lie of the sexual-freedom revolution is that you have to follow you sexual preference (whatever it is), that you have no choice. If I fall in love with someone, it's inevitable we'll end up in bed—unless I am a repressed and unhappy individual determined to stay in an unhappy marriage. If you feel attracted to other men, you will either "stay in the closet," repressed and unhappy, or you will enter the free-flowering splendor of the gay community.

> "The sexual focus of our lives is meant to be the opposite sex."

But this is sheer nonsense. It's really just a variation on the old line a guy gives who wants to take a girl to bed: "Fate meant us to be together. It's bigger than both of us. It's chemistry." One difference between human beings and animals is that we can control our sexuality; it doesn't have to control us. If we all did everything we felt like doing, the world would be sheer chaos. Instead, as rational, thinking creatures, we take our many desires into consideration—desires for sexual release, for personal intimacy, for long-lasting friendships, for marriage and children, for many things—and we decide on a course. We choose a lifestyle that really suits us. We may need to say no to certain desires, but the overall result will be positive, fitting our personal needs.

Temptations

Scripture does not indicate that it is wrong to be tempted. In fact, temptations are normal. The fact that you are tempted to have sexual relations with other men may reflect badly on our sex-crazed society, which inflames our tendencies, or it may reflect badly on your family background, as some psychologists say. I don't see that it reflects badly on you. How you came by the desires that trouble you I do not know. I suspect that most people feel a certain amount of sexual ambiguity, some people more than others.

I get many letters from young people who are afraid they are homosexuals. They've never lived a gay lifestyle, but they feel some variance in their sexual longings—maybe the opposite sex does not attract them in the way they expect is normal, or maybe they have tender feelings for a friend of the same sex. The gay movement claims that one out of ten people is a homosexual and that if you are one you can't do a thing about it. So the question arises: "Am I one?" Once the idea is planted, it tends to grow. And if a person tries it out, he will probably find that, indeed, he can be sexually aroused by his own sex. Therefore, he thinks, he must be gay. In reality, he may merely be ambivalent. In another society, in another time, he would have channeled his sexual desires in a different direction. Sexuality is more fluid than the gay movement leads people to believe. Sexual attraction is as much mental as physical.

Choose Your Lifestyle

You cannot choose your desires, but you can choose your lifestyle. As you say, your feelings and desires for sex will still be there. But what does that prove? Mine are still there too, but I have chosen to focus them within the marriage relationship. That means saying yes to some desires and no to a great many others. Some Christians are single, and they live with continuing heterosexual or homosexual desires. Need they be unhappy? The Bible answers a resounding no! The single, celibate life is honored in the New Testament without reservation. Everyone is called to it for some portion of his or her life. Some are called to it permanently. Jesus was, Paul possibly was, and countless other great and inspiring Christians through the ages have been celibate. Jesus' words in Matthew 19:12 suggest that the call to singleness is not always based on great religious feeling. Practical factors enter: "For some are eunuchs because they were born that way; others were made that way by men; and others have renounced marriage because of the kingdom of heaven." All three causes are honorable.

I believe singleness is the healthy and blessed lifestyle for you at this point. It won't be sheer bliss—I don't know of any lifestyle that is, realistically. And because your struggles are less acceptable in our society than mine, you will suffer a special loneliness in them. Given the judgmental disgust that many people feel regarding homosexuality, you can't expect the sympathies of vast numbers of people. However, you can hope to find the help and support of some.

Don't exaggerate the difficulty of sharing your situation privately with concerned, caring Christians. Many will not be able to accept and understand your situation, but many others will. I know some Christians who would be delighted to commit themselves to regular prayer and encouragement for someone in your shoes.

You cannot change your lifestyle alone. That is why I strongly encourage you to begin today asking God to put before you one or more people whom you can confide in with complete confidence. You need them not just to listen to you and accept you, but to play an active, caring part in your life, meeting regularly with you for prayer and Bible study. You need to take the risk of revealing your inner thoughts so that you can quit living in lonely secretiveness and begin to develop satisfying, deep relationships. Jesus is the answer to all our problems, but he doesn't work in a purely spiritual way. He has a physical and relational reality, what the Bible calls the "body of Christ"—that is, the church.

I look for the day when Christians will get over their homophobia and realize that those with homosexual temptations differ very little from the rest of us. We all struggle with temptations, and the Bible never treats one sin as worse than another. In the fellowship of the Holy Spirit, which is the togetherness binding Christians, we come closest to grasping Christ's full and final victory over sin.

You Can Change
There is no mysterious, awesome power in homosexual temptations. Temptation is temptation—we all know how impossible it can be when we are in the wrong situation and how easy to resist when we leave that situation. You

say you are not sure that you want to change. I think you do want to change, but you are not sure you can. The gay movement says that you cannot, that you can only repress your natural feelings. That is not so. It is most natural to follow Jesus. You were made to do that.

Chapter 2

Thinking About Virginity

The Importance of Virginity

Tara Bonaparte

Virgins used to receive a lot more respect for their decision to save themselves for marriage, writes Tara Bonaparte. She believes virgins still deserve that respect. In her opinion, virginity is the most precious gift you can give to someone. There are too many consequences associated with being sexually active to risk having sex before you're ready, she notes. She concludes that you'll appreciate sex more if you wait until you're with someone you truly love. Bonaparte is a teen who writes for *Foster Care Youth United*, a magazine for youth in the New York City foster care system.

Wuz up, people!!!! Well, this is the high yellow, big mouth, funny writer who comes correct with all the facts, coming at ya with an article that is strictly for the ladies. (But guys, feel free to read too.)

This article may help you understand some of the stresses that we ladies have to go through in being virgins. And ladies, this article may help you to understand things about yourselves.

This article can also speak to male virgins. The same way that some females have to worry about males, males also need to

Reprinted from "Virgin Power," by Tara Bonaparte, *Foster Care Youth United*, January/February 1999. Reprinted with permission from Youth Communications.

worry about some females. Because there are a lot of girls (and you girls know who you are) who want to take away the virginity from the last batch of virgin males that exists.

When my mother and father were growing up, it was a good thing for a girl to be a virgin. My grandparents made sure that all of their five daughters (including my mom) ran around claiming what was between their legs was 14 carat gold. My grandparents always let their daughters know the importance of being a virgin. And that is why I know the importance of being a virgin.

No Respect

Today it seems as if nobody has any respect for themselves. Girls (not all of them) are running around having sex with any and every boy who says they love them.

And the boys. I just have no words. They are running around reproducing more children than rabbits. Having sex with any girl who has a big butt and a nice smile.

Where did the respect for being a virgin go?

Being a teenager, I know that one of the biggest things that teens worry about is self-image. We teenagers are always worried about what our friends think. We're always trying to be down with the latest craze.

And when I look around, the newest craze is for people to talk about all the sex they have. And if you happen to be that one teenager who hasn't experienced the "wonder" of having sex, it can be very difficult.

Name Calling

"Man, you ain't had sex yet?"

"You scared or something?"

"What, are you gay?"

If you are a virgin, these statements are probably very familiar to you. Most of the time they come from your friends, but sometimes they even come from your partner. These statements can make the strongest person feel like an idiot.

Well, let me shine some light on these problems.

If you've heard these comments from a friend, then there are some things that you really need to know. Ninety-nine percent of the time your friend is lying about her own sex experience. And liars always try to make themselves look good by putting others down.

> Being a virgin is the most precious thing in the universe.

Does your friend usually bring up the topic of sex when he/she is around a large group of people? If your friend does, then I'm sorry to say that he/she is probably still a virgin too. Because if a person is having sex, there is no need to brag about it.

If you've heard those statements from your partner, there is only one reason he/she is telling you that. He/she is obviously trying to make you feel bad that you're a virgin. Bad enough to give it up to him/her.

Don't be fooled, because if your partner really loved you, then he/she wouldn't be trying to make you rush into a serious, life or death decision. And believe me, it is.

Be Sure

To all the virgins out there—if your mama or daddy didn't tell you this, then I think that it is time that we have "The Talk." So to everyone who is reading this article, take these words as seriously as the air that you are breathing.

To me, being a virgin is the most precious thing in the universe. And when I finally do decide to lose my virginity, it will be when I'm ready. And when I'm in love.

Don't let anyone pressure you into doing anything that you don't want to do. And please don't be fooled by those silly lines like "I have needs" or "It will make our relationship grow stronger."

Give me a break. Everyone makes sex seem like a holiday in the Bahamas, but nobody bothers to explain the consequences. And there are plenty.

Party's Over

Sex (if done right) can be a beautiful thing. But everything is not beautiful about sex. So, to that young virgin who is about to take that first step to sex—listen up. I don't care where you are either. You could be at your boyfriend's/girlfriend's buck naked and just happen to pick up this article. You better get your clothes and run.

Just like they say that weed is a gateway drug, sex can lead to a baby or a serious disease. And virgins can get pregnant the very first time they have sex.

Teens Are Remaining Virgins Longer

- In 1995, 50% of girls and women aged 15 to 19 had had sex, down from 55% in 1990.
- 55% of single males aged 15 to 19 have had sex, down from 60% in 1988.
- 70% of 18- and 19-year-old women have had sex, down from 74% in 1990.
- 38% of girls aged 15 to 17 have had sex, down from 41% in 1990.
- The average age at which teens have their first sexual experience has risen from 15.8 in 1997 to 16.3 in 1998.

National Center for Health Statistics, Urban Institute, Durex Global Survey.

There was this one girl I knew when I was younger. Her name was Taisha. She was pretty, smart and funny. Everyone wanted to be just like her. Every time my family and I played house, I would be her. She was 18 and still a virgin. I was seven and still believed in the stork. But still, I always told everyone that Taisha was my best friend.

When I reached 12, I knew all I needed to know about sex. I knew that I could get pregnant. I also knew about AIDS. I guess Taisha didn't know. The last I heard she was 25, had AIDS and was pregnant for her third time. And I heard that her children have the AIDS virus. Not everyone can pass on the AIDS virus to their children, and I was hoping that she didn't pass it on to hers. But she did. Sad, isn't it?

Her First Time

Taisha's cousin told me that the first person she had sex with gave her the AIDS virus. So don't sit there and say, "It can't happen to me." Because as long as there are teenagers and sex out there, it can happen to you.

You could be having sex for 50 years (even though the thought is very scary) and never catch a disease. Or you can have sex just once and end up with the AIDS virus. So be careful.

> There are a lot of good things about making love. But don't be in such a rush to find out what's so good.

Along with babies and diseases, sex also gives you a reputation. And once you gain a reputation, it is going to stick with you for a long time. You could have the reputation of a "goodie two shoes," but all it takes is for you to have sex with one not-so-special person to be labeled a h-e. And I know that isn't right, but unfortunately that is the world that we are living in today.

To be honest, a boy is not really going to be called anything but "The man" for having sex. So ladies, you and your boyfriend can have sex, but only you will get the bad reputation. Hmmm, something to think about.

Making Love

Now, at this point, I know you are probably saying, "Damn, this girl is trying to keep our legs closed forever."

Well, that is not completely true. I'm just trying to make sure that before anyone goes out and does something as serious as sex, they should know about the good and the bad.

There are a lot of good things about making love. But don't be in such a rush to find out what's so good. Because the longer you wait, the more you will appreciate sex when you finally have it. And you will appreciate it more if it's with somebody you really love. So people, let me end this article with a little advice.

Make your decision right, because it could change the rest of your life.

Deciding to Wait

Lilybird

One reason why many teens decide to have sex is because they're simply curious about the experience. Lilybird is a teenager who was anxious to lose her virginity before she became "too old"; however, she wants her first time to be with someone special. In her quest to lose her virginity, Lilybird began to change her ideas about being a virgin until she realized that sex will have a lot more meaning for her if she waits until she's in love and is emotionally ready. Lilybird is a teen writer for *Foster Care Youth United*, a magazine written by and for teens in the New York City foster care system.

The way I felt about my virginity was I wanted to lose it before I got too old, but I didn't wanna lose it to just anybody. When I spoke to my friends about it they would say, "Girl, you're stupid, I wish I was a virgin," or "I wish I waited." But I felt like they didn't understand because it wasn't their problem. I wanted to know what it was like before I got too old.

I'm 16 and for a while I thought I was waiting too long. I didn't know what the right time was, so I wanted to lose it quick before it was too late. In some ways I thought that by having sex I would mature and not be the same little girl.

Reprinted from "My Virginity: I Wanted to Lose It Quick," by Lilybird, *Foster Care Youth United,* March/April 1996. Reprinted with permission from Youth Communications.

I had been in situations where I was about to have sex, but I was so scared my whole body was shaking. I was scared of exposing my body to a guy and finding out later that I didn't know him well enough.

Not Wanting to Rush

People would always say to me "It's alright to be nervous," or "It's normal to be a 16-year-old virgin." But teenagers now are expected to grow up a lot faster than teenagers in the past.

Getting a man was not the problem, it was finding the right one. I didn't wanna rush into anything and later say to myself, "I should never have lost it to him."

I also was worried that the word would get out that I was "sexin' this brotha" and I'd get treated like a chicken around my way. I've seen it happen to mad girls and I refuse to let it happen to me. In my neighborhood, when guys find out you're having sex, they hound you like you're raw meat.

When someone asks me if I'm a virgin, I'm not ashamed to admit I am. But when they want more detail, I get embarrassed because they probably think I'm hot in the pants.

> I wanted to lose [my virginity] quick before it was too late.

I began to think of my virginity as a big problem around the time one of my good friends lost it last year. After that, it was on my mind non-stop. I felt like if I didn't lose it, my friend and I would have nothing to talk about and she would eventually outgrow me.

Too Scared

I had boyfriends who I could have lost it to, but they weren't the right guys and I would have regretted it.

For example, there was this guy Jaquan. He and I weren't really serious from the get, so I wasn't gonna do anything with him. Besides, he knows mad people around my way. If I had done something with him, news would have gotten out.

I remember one time I was going out with this guy Richard. We were in his room making out and it started to go further. I wanted to, but I was too scared to expose my body. He asked me if I was alright.

> I felt like if I didn't lose [my virginity], my friend and I would have nothing to talk about and she would eventually outgrow me.

I jumped off his bed with the quickness and made up some excuse about how I was hungry and wanted to go to the store. I think he knew I was scared because he didn't push the issue. We went to the store, he walked me to the bus stop, then I went home.

I was kicking myself when I got on the bus. I had wanted it for so long but when I had the opportunity I got scared. I felt like I was gonna make a fool of myself. I know now that having sex with him would have been a mistake, because he and I didn't last that long. I would have felt used.

As months passed I started to change my ideas about being a virgin. I looked around and saw what happened to some girls who rushed into having sex, or girls who caught STD's from their man messin' around on them.

I know one girl who got played by her man. He told her to stop calling him, saying "You're too immature," and even called her a hoe. She still kept stressing him. Her close friend had sex and she wanted to try it out so bad, she did it with a guy who she knew was not faithful to her.

A New Attitude

I think God made an example of her to help me see the light, because I don't want to get played like that. I feel there are other things I can think about, like my clothes and hair, rather than sex. After a while it got to the point where I had to say to myself, "Why are you stressin' it so much?"

My friends talk about sex like it's regular and boring because they've been doing it for so long and so much. I don't want it to become regular for me at such a young age, for it to become "just sex." That's why I say to myself now, "When I get older and finally do it, I'm gonna have a lot more thrills in my life than the ones who already went through it."

I don't know if time has changed my whole perspective on this issue, or seeing other teenage sexual relationships gone bad. For some reason "having sex" doesn't seem as big and over-powering as before. Its kind of like money in the bank—the longer you wait, the more loot you'll have because of interest.

It's Better to Wait

I want to wait to find the right guy. Not just some guy who looks mad good, is nice only when he's not drunk, and mad funny. I need to know he is mature emotionally, not just physically. Some guys think just because they've had a lot of partners, they're mature enough to handle sex. Anybody can have sex, but not everyone can handle sex. Waiting until you're married to me is kind of long, but having sex just because it might be going out of style is crazy.

So, it's still on my mind but not like before. As time passed I realized that life is not gonna end just because I'm not having sex yet. There's other things I can do with my boyfriends. Virginity should be given to someone you care about or love, and he should feel the same for you.

Alternatives to Intercourse

Tara McCarthy

There are lots of ways that you can express your sexuality without having sexual intercourse. Below, Tara McCarthy explains how she is able to remain a virgin yet still have an active sex life. During a re-examination of her sexual past, McCarthy discovered that sexual play has more meaning for her if she's with someone she cares about. She's proud that she has stayed true to her ideals so she can give her future husband the gift of her virginity. McCarthy is a freelance writer who writes about teen and women's issues.

I've always hated that Madonna song "Like a Virgin"—the "touched for the very first time" bit, in particular—because at 26, *I'm* still a virgin, and I've been touched, kissed, prodded, rubbed, caressed, licked, nibbled—you name it. More times than I'd like to admit. I don't fit the image of a virgin except for one salient fact: I've never had sexual intercourse.

A Life Without Sex

I am not a religious fanatic or a prude. I'm not a wallflower, nor have I ever had any trouble finding guys who wanted to sleep

Excerpted from *Been There, Haven't Done That,* by Tara McCarthy. Copyright ©1996 by Tara McCarthy. Reprinted with permission from Warner Books, Inc.

with me. I go to movies and concerts. I have good days and bad days at pool. I buy a lot of CDs. I have a life.

The decision to have a life without having premarital sex isn't an easy one, but I made it a long time ago and have had few regrets. It would be convenient to say that I decided to wait because of AIDS; not having sex because you fear for your health is somehow easier for people to understand. But my decision was made before I'd even heard of AIDS, so disease was not the deterrent. Maybe my decision was made *for* me, to an extent, when my mother stood at our kitchen sink peeling a cucumber, of all things, and told 10-year-old me that sex is something that two people do when they really love each other.

For years I waited with great anticipation for my attitude to change. I knew that Catholic girls were supposed to go nuts when they got to college. Alas, four years at Harvard passed without any change in my sexual status. After graduation I moved to Dublin, landed a job at a music magazine and felt I was truly living my own life for the first time. It was such a rock-and-roll life—I frequented pubs and clubs and spent nights with spiky-haired synthesizer players—it only made sense that having sex would follow.

What stopped me? The same reasoning that kept me from sleeping with a long-term serious boyfriend when I returned to the States: Since intercourse is the only thing that can get you pregnant and the only act that physically joins two people together, I've imbued it with symbolic meaning and reserved a special place for it in my life. I've allowed myself other physical pleasures for reasons that are equally clear—I'm human, I have sexual impulses and I don't see anything wrong with acting on them.

> At 26, I'm still a virgin, and I've been touched, kissed, prodded, rubbed, caressed, licked, nibbled—you name it.

Truth is, I've had very satisfying, very intimate physical and emotional relationships with men in my life. Sure, I've left some of them hanging, but not as a general rule. A lot of people think that I've come so close I might as well have done it, that my cut off point is completely arbitrary, and that therefore I'm not *really* a virgin. Well, if the words *chaste* and *pure* enter into your definition of *virgin,* I would never claim to be one. I'm probably more in tune with what I like and don't like in bed than a woman who has slept with one or two guys and hasn't really fooled around with anyone else.

> There's so much emphasis on intercourse that people aren't given the chance to figure out what else there is and how to be a sexual being without having actual sex.

But if you get caught up in semantics you miss my point, which is that the traditional definition of virginity is pretty outdated. You can venture far beyond innocent goodnight kisses on the front porch and explore your sexuality without risking pregnancy, disease and your sense of self.

Too Much Emphasis on Intercourse

A boyfriend once told me that if his parents knew what we did in bed together, they'd probably wish we were just having sex. What's that all about? I don't own handcuffs. I'm not a contortionist. But society shies away from anything that isn't standard missionary-position screwing. There's so much emphasis on intercourse that people aren't given the chance to figure out what else there is and how to be a sexual being without having actual sex. We forget that two people can enjoy each other's bodies—and their own—with less risk.

Of course, sex will never be risk-free. People make mistakes, and I'm no exception, but the best ones are those you can learn from and promptly forget, not the ones that you have to put through college.

Some of my own worst missteps involved not being honest about who I am and what I want out of life and romance. When

The Benefits of Outercourse

You're not saying no to sex when you practice Outercourse. You're saying *oh, God, yes* to all the things that get overlooked when you fall into an intercourse rut (as it were). Below, five Outercourse aficionados speak out. Their true tales might make true believers of you.

• "My fiancé and I decided to follow the advice from a sex book and not have intercourse, or even oral sex, for a while. We just touched, talked, groped. I went from not having orgasms to having them all the time. Now, when I look at other couples and wonder if they're having the great sex we're having, I feel smug!"—Jennifer, 27, graduate student, Seattle

• "To have good sex, you have to let your guard down. It's hard not to be embarrassed about doing things like dry humping. Once you do, it's like being a teenager again and having all this sexual energy and not knowing what to do with it."—Cara, 25, account executive, Minneapolis

• "We waited four months to have intercourse. I said I wasn't ready for a commitment, but really, I just knew that the holding back was more exciting for me. It was like, 'The suspense is killing me; I hope it lasts.'"—Heather, 24, caterer, Middlebury VT

• "We don't want sex to be routine. My boyfriend and I waited until we couldn't take it any longer before we finally had sex. Now we'll sometimes go without intercourse for a week. I'm a romantic. I don't want it to be ordinary."—Elizabeth, 24, researcher, New York City

• "I was raised Catholic. So I held off on intercourse for as long as I could. My friends who were having sex didn't have orgasms, but I did, all the time. Even now that I'm not a virgin, there's something special about holding off—once you have intercourse, the mystery is gone. Restraint is exciting."—Andrea, 27, model booker, New York City

Suzanna Markstein, *Mademoiselle*, October 1996.

I somehow got on the subject of sex with Bill,* a musician I'd met in Belfast—OK, it came up because we were in bed together—I told him that I had had very few relationships involving sex in the past (wild understatement). Later, he asked me playfully to tell him the strangest place I had ever done it, and I considered making something up but blanked.

> A part of me has always felt that my virginity set me apart.

"I can't answer that question," I began, "because I've never had sex . . ."

I thought about adding "in any strange places," which would have been perfectly true. But I couldn't do it, so there it was, just hanging out there: "I've never had sex . . ."

"But you were just talking about relationships where sex had been involved."

Caught.

Ah yes, I attempted, but only in the sense that it had been brought up, discussed and decided against.

"What are you, saving yourself for marriage or something?" he asked. All of a sudden I felt ridiculous.

An Exception to the Norm

Not because *waiting* was ridiculous, but because attempting to dodge the subject of my virginity was a ridiculous thing for me to be doing. I knew how much of an exception to the norm I was, and that my virginity made me less attractive in some men's eyes. The fact that I went to an Ivy League college had had the same effect in certain situations; a temp agent once told me to take Harvard off my resume because it would hurt my chances of getting a summer job as a secretary. I could have lied—sparing potential employers the "Harvard" and potential boyfriends the "virgin"—but what was the point if all it got me was a job I didn't want and a guy who didn't want the real me?

* All names have been changed.

These days, the embarrassment factor—such a huge part of the virgin experience—is gone. I know that for me, the right time, place, guy and circumstances have yet to coincide. I'm hardly going to isolate myself from the world or lie to it in the meantime.

When will it happen? Maybe not for some time, given the fact that my selection of single men is somewhat limited. I believe so strongly that sexual intercourse is not to be taken lightly that it's impossible for me to have a relationship with someone who doesn't feel the same. I sometimes wish there were more potential partners for me to choose from, but I'm not bitter—unlike Dan,* a fellow virgin I used to know. When I last saw him, he went on and on about how the world would be a better place if there were more people "like us," and I suddenly realized why virgins so often get a bad rap. Not only was Dan unbearably self-righteous—as many vocal virgins in the media tend to be—but he appeared to be carrying an enormous chip on his shoulder.

> The physical pleasure isn't nearly so important to me as the emotional release of giving myself to someone—the right one—body and soul.

Like a Tattoo

For all my frustrations with not having found the right person, a part of me has always felt that my virginity set me apart, and not necessarily in a negative way—more like a cool tattoo on an obscure body part. In fact, virginity and tattoos have a lot in common. Getting rid of them often proves difficult and painful. And just as a skull and crossbones, an I Love Mom or a simple rose tattoo can mean different things to different people, the way we view our virginity—and losing it—is unique to each of us (so much so that Hallmark could put out a line of cards for the occasion, ranging from "Happy Hump Day" to "We're sorry for your loss"). I imagine Dan saw his virginity as an actual cross to bear, something the whole world could see and pass judgment on. Mine I've often seen as an anchor tattoo, perhaps hidden away on an ankle or butt cheek. Something that grounded me when other aspects of my life were out of control. Something that would one day give way and let me set sail.

I considered raising anchor with my most recent boyfriend, Mark.* We'd met in passing several years before, but our relationship really started while he was living in Sweden, finishing research for his master's degree. In the course of a 10-month correspondence, Mark and I went from being friends to lovers, and when he moved to New York City we became an established couple. That isn't to say we were perfectly compatible. Take our romantic histories: Mark could count on his fingers the dates he'd had, while I'd need an abacus. He was in love with all of the women he'd had sex with, and he simply couldn't fathom how I could have been intimate with so many guys I didn't care for deeply.

A Re-Examination

Mark's questions forced me to reexamine my sexual history, and I found that I wasn't so thrilled with it either. I'd always felt, on some level, that resisting intercourse made up for all my flings. But looking back, it seemed that in my search for the right man, I'd gone places and done things I would no longer feel comfortable doing. It took loving and being loved by Mark, someone who understood my ideals but challenged whether I'd really lived up to them, to help me realize that, intercourse aside, I don't want to be doing *anything* sexual with just anybody.

> When I do decide to have sex, it will be the biggest gift I've ever given anyone in my life.

I no longer feel that need to find "the one" with such urgency, in no small part due to the way in which Mark and I eventually ended our year-plus romantic involvement. Agreeing that we would be better off as friends felt like the most mature decision I'd ever made in my love life. Now that I've reached that level of maturity, I don't think there's any going back. I know what I want and I still believe it's out there, but until I find it, I simply can't see myself hooking up with random men or fooling around with a guy I've only had a few dates with. It's not who I want to be.

It's possible that when all is said and done and my first real lover has fallen asleep beside me, I'll lie there and say to myself, "You idiot, you could have been doing that for years!" But I don't have any romanticized notions of the mechanics of intercourse. In spite of an ever-increasing desire for what I imagine it feels like, I'm not expecting a mind-blowing orgasm or the best sexual experience of my life. The physical pleasure isn't nearly so important to me as the emotional release of giving myself to someone—the right one—body and soul.

The Biggest Gift

For a long time I was looking for someone worthy, someone who understood and deserved a gift of this magnitude. But that feeling of superiority has been replaced over the years with a quieter sense of power and pride at having stuck to my guns.

I know, simply, that it will happen with someone who loves me and whom I love back—unreservedly. I also know that when I do decide to have sex, it will be the biggest gift I've ever given anyone in my life. It just took me a long time to understand that I'd be giving it to myself.

A Born-Again Virgin

David Erikson

For many years, David Erikson, a freelance writer, believed that if the sexual chemistry was right between him and his sexual partner, then love and intimacy would follow. He discovered, however, that the lack of emotional bonds between him and his partners just led to meaningless sex and feelings of loneliness. The way to make sex meaningful, he has decided, is to build the emotional bonds first. He has resolved to abstain from sex until he's willing to give his body and soul to his one true love on his wedding night.

We started kissing just outside her door, our hands feeling through coats and shirts and sweaters. "Why don't you come in?" my date whispered, making it clear that sex was there for the asking. But I didn't ask; I walked away.

"What? No sex?" my buddies said, stunned. "Man, you'd better think that over." I have. But casual sex—while exciting for about, oh, 15 minutes—has never given me what I really want. I want something that lasts past bagels and cream cheese in the morning. I want a relationship that's laced with intimacy, trust—and no sex until we're married.

I've tried it both ways. (Who would listen to me if I hadn't?) In college, my weekends revolved around the hook-up scene, and the first step in most relationships was testing our chemistry in bed. I figured that if the sex was good, the rest—communication, humor, maybe even *love*—would follow. But instead of being the start of something fulfilling and intertwining, sex always left me feeling lonelier than before.

The Facts About Secondary Virginity

Right now you are probably thinking, "Why do I want to be a virgin? When I was a virgin I was dying to lose it, why should I find it now?" There are some benefits from being a virgin that you probably haven't considered.

• Orgasms experienced by recovered virgins are 200% stronger than those by non-virgins.

• After regaining their virginity, 34.8% of the users claimed that food tasted better. . . .

• The death rate among virgins is 300% lower than that among non-virgins. . . .

• Virgins are 86.1% less likely to get into hazardous automobile accidents. . . .

• Hair loss is 45.6% less prevalent among male virgins than non-virgins.

• 67% of all American Olympians are virgins.

• Mother Theresa *and* the Pope are virgins.

• Extensive testing has shown weight loss is substantially easier while you are a virgin.

• Donald Trump first started off as a virgin.

Society for the Recapture of Virginity, Inc., www.thebluedot.com/srv/facts.html

---

Flashback to the instant this truth hit home for me: It was our third date, and we lay naked in bed, laughing, tickling . . . you get the picture. In the immediate moment after the immediate sex, I realized that I barely knew the woman next to me. What was her middle name? Her favorite color? Did she have a good singing voice?

Not long after that night, filled with maybe 900 seconds of thrill, we broke up. I suppose we could have continued to just do it for several months until we finally admitted it wasn't going to work. But things somehow felt wrong between us. No doubt other flaws plagued our romance, too—but the fact that our physical relationship had jumped way ahead of anything we were ready for emotionally seemed to amplify our rifts and harm our chances to mend them. Ultimately, I just couldn't find a way to bridge the chasm between the intimacy of our sex life and the hollowness of our conversations.

> Casual sex—while exciting for about, oh, 15 minutes—has never given me what I really want.

That was when I stopped laughing off abstinence—a concept that had always conjured up images of God as the Great Cosmic Killjoy. Perhaps, I began to think, the no-sex-before-marriage rule was more than a centuries-old joke. Maybe it wasn't so much a barrier designed to keep me from something good as a boundary set in place to guide me to something *better.* Maybe there was something contradictory about the fact that I'd given my body to someone, but kept parts of my heart and soul to myself. The more I thought about it, the more I saw the logic and beauty of total union—no holds barred—and, for me, that meant waiting for sex until marriage.

Dating Sans Sex

Sometimes I wonder if I've lost my mind. Believe me, plenty of women would agree with that theory. "You're on a power trip," one date told me, insisting (in the middle of a crowded restaurant, I might add) that my whole celibacy deal was nothing more than a way to show off my superior will.

"You won't have sex? That's bullshit! You're just scared," another said. (So much for the stereotype that men want to screw and women crave endless foreplay.) But let me assure anyone still with me here, I'm not trying to be a male tease. It's just that I dream of saving my sexual energies for one woman.

Worth the Wait

I often fantasize about my wedding night. The entire ordeal of the ceremony, reception, dancing and thank-you's is over, and at last I'm alone with my wife. I dream that this night will be amazing, and that dream helps me wait. But what if the sex isn't mind-blowingly wonderful? Won't I be sorry I didn't find out before it was too late? Sometimes that worries me. I've decided, though, that the most important thing about our relationship will be our spiritual and emotional connection—after all, that's what will keep us in love with each other long after the passion fades. If we build our commitment on a deeper level, then sex will be a wonderful bonus. Then we can truly say we're making love.

Point of Contention: Will Abstinence-Only Sex Education Programs Reduce Teen Sex?

In 1996, concern over the high teen pregnancy rate led Congress to allocate $50 million over five years to states that agreed to teach abstinence-only education programs in the nation's public schools. Schools that accepted the funds must teach students that premarital sex and sex outside of marriage are frowned upon by society, and that the only guaranteed way to prevent pregnancy and sexually transmitted diseases is through abstinence. Supporters of the abstinence-only programs contend that comprehensive sex education programs—which teach teens about contraception and how to protect themselves from STDs—essentially give teens permission to have sex. They claim that teens are less likely to have sex if they're told that premarital sex is unacceptable. Opponents argue that these abstinence-only programs don't work. They say that teens are going to have sex no matter what they're told, therefore, it's better to teach them how to avoid the consequences, such as pregnancy and STDs.

The two viewpoints presented here offer both sides of this debate. Ellen Goodman is a syndicated columnist. Joseph Perkins is an editorial writer for the *San Diego Union-Tribune*.

Yes: Abstinence-Only Sex Education Will Reduce Teen Sex

Joseph Perkins

Alexandra Stevenson, a recent graduate of La Jolla Country Day School, raised a lot of eyebrows when she made it all the way to the Wimbledon semifinals. And the 18-year-old almost certainly raised as many eyebrows when she recently revealed in a nationally televised interview that she has never been kissed.

Indeed, it's one thing for a teen-ager to make an overnight transition from a promising high school tennis player to a serious contender for a Grand Slam tennis title. But to think that she made it all the way through high school without having sex, without having so much as a kiss. Forget about it.

Well, as it happens, young Alexandra is not such an aberration. In fact, an increasing number of her fellow teens are also practicing chastity. And much of the credit for this must go to the growing number of abstinence-only programs that are reaching youngsters throughout the country.

The teen-abstinence movement got a major boost by the 1996 welfare reform law, which included a provision setting aside $250 million over five years for a federal program to discourage teen sex.

The ground rules of the program are to teach younger Americans "the social, psychological and health gains to be realized by abstaining from sexual activity" and to caution teens that "sexual activity outside of . . . marriage is likely to have harmful psychological and physical effects."

States can get a share of the federal money by putting up

$3 for every $4 they request from Washington. The maximum yearly grant a state may receive is $5.7 million, which the state must match with $4.2 million of its own.

> If teens get the message that underage, premarital sex is not normative, . . . then youngsters will be less inclined to have sex.

Over the past two years, the states have created nearly 700 new abstinence-only programs, bringing the nationwide total to roughly 1,000. And even the lone state government that has chosen not to participate in the federal program, California, is funding abstinence-only programs out of state coffers.

This represents a radical shift in public policy with respect to teens and sex. For the past quarter-century, at least, the prevailing wisdom has been that the government ought not waste time and tax dollars trying to discourage the underaged from having sex.

The more "realistic" and "sensible" approach, the thinking went, was for the government to bend its efforts to preventing unwanted pregnancies and sexually transmitted diseases by supporting programs that make condoms and birth control pills more readily available to youngsters.

Well, this "teens-will-be-teens" orthodoxy has not withered away by any stretch of the imagination, but it does face a serious challenge today from the abstinence-only movement. And this challenge has the "sex education" crowd (which teaches chastity as one of several sexual "options" for kids) plenty worried.

And with good cause. The abstinence-only movement is producing desired results. Indeed, since federal funds started flowing to abstinence-only programs in 1997, the number of teen-age pregnancies, abortions and births have fallen. Moreover, the average age at which youngsters have their first sexual experience has risen from 15.8 in 1997 to 16.3 in 1998, according to the Durex Global Survey.

These developments show that the prevailing wisdom about teen sex—that kids simply cannot control their raging hormones, that they are bound to have sex—is a fallacy. Kids live up or down to expectations.

Indeed, if adults impart the message to teens that they are expected to be sexually active, that it's OK as long as they use a condom or take the pill, then those teens are that much more likely to engage in sexual activity.

On the other hand, if teens get the message that underage, premarital sex is not normative, that adults will not tacitly condone teen promiscuity by providing contraceptives-on-demand, no questions asked, then youngsters will be less inclined to have sex.

There are millions of responsible teens out there, like Alexandra Stevenson, who are living proof that younger Americans are quite capable of waiting at least until they are adults before becoming sexually active.

They recognize that the best way to avoid unwanted pregnancies and sexually transmitted diseases is not by practicing so-called "safe sex"—by using condoms and birth control pills—but by refraining from sex altogether.

Reprinted from "The Best Choice for Teens Concerning Sex," by Joseph Perkins, *The San Diego Union-Tribune*, August 13, 1999. Reprinted with permission from the author.

No: Abstinence-Only Sex Education Programs Will Not Reduce Teen Sex

Ellen Goodman

I have always had a soft spot for the folks who preach abstinence. For one thing, I like their rap lines. You know, "Pet Your Dog, Not Your Date." "Do the Right Thing, Wait for the Ring."

Reprinted by permission of Kirk Anderson.

Then, too, they were also the ones who came up with the idea of "Secondary Virginity," which is a kind of biological annulment. This prompted a young lawyer in my family to ask, "Can you have a third or a fourth virginity? Or is it two strikes and you're out?"

In any case, I can happily agree with the rightest wing of this movement in lamenting the number of kids who start having sex far too young and far too unhappily with far too many consequences. Do teens need help saying no when all the messages around them, from media to partners, are saying yes, yes, yes? Do they need adults to talk with them about waiting? Sure.

Abstinence Only
Why then do I find myself queasy when the government offers to pass out some $50 million a year for educational pro-

grams that will teach abstinence only? Try the word "only."

In one of those after-hours maneuvers for which Washington is famous, a provision offering money for abstinence-only programs was snuck into the 1996 welfare reform bill.

The logic that welded abstinence to welfare was that unwed teen moms often end up on AFDC. No sex, no teen moms. Ergo no welfare. Teach kids abstinence and nothing but abstinence.

Under the guidelines, any approved government program must have "as its exclusive purpose, teaching the social, psychological and health gains to be realized by abstaining from sexual activity." Exactly which sexual "activity" to be avoided—masturbation? French-kissing?—remains undefined.

But the guidelines do clearly say that kids must be taught that sex is only for marriage. Despite the fact that 90 percent of Americans—including parents and members of Congress—had their first sex outside of marriage, abstinence-only teaches that married intercourse is "the expected standard of human sexual activity."

> There's no reliable evidence that current abstinence-only programs reduce sexual activity.

To get government money, a program must even teach that unmarried sex is "likely to have harmful psychological and physical effects."

If that sounds like legislated fear-mongering, a recent California study of abstinence programs bears it out.

In one "educational" video, a student asks what happens if he wants to have sex before marriage. The instructor answers, "Well, I guess you'll just have to be prepared to die."

If the idea of federally funded disinformation is troubling enough, the lack of information is worse. Under these guidelines, abstinence-only programs can't teach about contraception. Nor talk openly and frankly about those banned "sexual activities." This "education" is monosyllabic.

I agree that abstinence should have a strong role in a comprehensive program. But this is all-or-nothing money, meant to replace any other programs, not enrich them with, say, an abstinence unit. The states have to find $3 for every $4 they get from Washington.

And there's no reliable evidence the current abstinence-only programs reduce sexual activity.

Today we know a fair amount about kids who have early, too early, intercourse. They're likely to be physically mature, to come from poor single-parent families. The kids who delay sex tend to have mentors, to read and write better, to have fewer stereotypes about sex roles, to be busy and connected. I still think the best abstinence program is an after-school program.

But now the states have to decide whether to ask for this hush money.

Just Say No

Debra Haffner of SIECUS, the Sex Information and Education Council of the United States, says, "We are giving states the same advice we are giving teens. Abstain, and if you are not going to abstain, act responsibly."

So far all but half a dozen states have caved to peer group pressure. Some states like Maine want to use the money for a media campaign. Others say they'll use it to teach just the youngest kids. Still others are trying to find a creative end run around the restrictions. But even those states will have to take money from another pot.

Money, especially federal money, can be awfully seductive. It's hard to just say no to government dollars. But this is one time when states should practice abstinence—and not preach it.

The Pressures Teens Face to Have Sex

Peer Pressure on Teenage Boys

Robin Chan

Boys often boast about their sexual conquests to their friends and ridicule their classmates who admit they are still virgins. In the following essay, Robin Chan writes that many boys are still virgins and proud of the fact. He notes that virgins don't have to worry about sexually transmitted diseases or their girlfriends getting pregnant and he urges teens not to give in to the peer pressure to have sex. Chan writes for *New Youth Connection*, a New York City magazine written by and for teens.

The names in this story have been changed.

One time in the boys locker room in the local YMCA, three guys who were changing clothes across from me and my friends started talking about who they had "done" the night before. Then they asked us who we had done. We told them we didn't do anyone because we were virgins. One of the guys rolled on the floor laughing while another one said, "They're virgins! HA-HA, they're little boys that get dressed up by mommy!"

A virgin is not an easy thing for a teenage guy to be. It seems like everywhere we turn, whether we're at the mall or watching

Reprinted from "Handling the Pressure," by Robin Chan, *New Youth Connection*, November 1996. Reprinted with permission from Youth Communications.

TV, something sex-related is going on. Sure we feel the pressure, sure we are curious to try it out, and sure we feel awkward talking about it when everyone around us says they're doing it.

Odd Men Out

We also know that we don't want to have sex yet. But people like those guys at the Y make it seem like being a virgin is a major crime or sin, that virgins are "losers" and not real men. Why can't they accept and respect the way we choose to be? If you're "doing it," good for you. You don't have to bring us into this when we're not ready.

I'm not the only teenage guy who's a virgin. I've interviewed some other guys who haven't had sex yet. Some feel ashamed that in this sex-crazed world, they're virgins. Others, like me, take pride, in the fact that we are who we are.

What's the Rush?

Most guys I interviewed had several reasons for abstaining from sex. Keith, 18, said, "My family wouldn't allow it." But he also said that he's just not ready for sex at his age. "When I'm 21, I'll know that I'm old enough for something like that," he told me. "My brother influenced my belief because he's a virgin and he's 24."

George, 16, of Bronx Science HS, feels the same way. "I'm too young to have sex," he said, adding that he believes in "sex after marriage."

> A virgin is not an easy thing for a guy to be.

Like George, Jim, 15, of Stuyvesant HS, believes in waiting until after marriage to have sex. "Besides," he said, "I feel safer not doing it." Jim feels that the risks and dangers of having sex, like AIDS, STD's, or getting a girl pregnant, are things he isn't ready to handle. "I choose to be a virgin because if anything bad happens, that's not good. I'm responsible."

Pressures and Temptations

But guys who want to wait often find that they don't get a lot of support. "We are pressured by friends and the stereotype that guys who have sex are macho and cool," said Nick, 15, of Bronx Science HS. Nick says he doesn't let this get to him but Keith admitted that it can be tough to stand up to all the pressures and temptations lurking out there.

"Sometimes I'm tormented by the fact that I'm a virgin," Keith said, "because when I see people around, and they say what they did, and I didn't do anything, I feel like the odd man out." Other guys will

> Don't give in to the pressure, don't have sex to impress someone and don't do it just to satisfy your curiosity.

also "say stupid things like, 'Your d-ck will fall off [if you don't have sex],' but I don't listen to those stupid things," Keith said.

It's not only other guys who can pressure you; women do it too. Keith told me about a woman he worked with who used to come on to him. "She would say, 'Step into my office' and she would start complimenting me. One time she tried to touch me, but I said to her, 'I don't play like that.'" The woman apologized but Keith still thinks the experience "was a little like sexual harassment."

It was easy for Keith to say no in this case, but what if it was a girlfriend that was pressuring him? Keith says that "from the beginning" he would tell any girl he was really interested in that "I don't want to have sex, I just want to have a nice relationship."

All these guys agree that, as Nick put it, "sex isn't mandatory in a relationship." Jim said, "[Sex] is not that important because a relationship is about love and caring about each other and other stuff." Keith feels that a relationship is about "being with a companion, a person to say words of compassion to," not about sex.

I hope this article will enlighten the people who think virgins are losers. I also hope it will make anyone who is considering having sex because they're sick of being pressured think twice about doing something they might regret or that will change their whole life forever.

Worth Waiting For

I thought that only other virgins would agree with me but I was wrong. One guy I talked to who is 17 and sexually active said, "Virgins are not losers. They are probably better people because they know what they want and when they want it." As Jim said, "We choose not to have [sex] yet because we are worth waiting for, like the commercial said."

So, to the other virgins out there, I say: Don't give in to the pressure, don't have sex to impress someone and don't do it just to satisfy your curiosity. Do it when you're good and ready.

As for me, right now I am more concerned about family, friends, school, the SAT, and my future. There'll be a time for me to have sex but it won't be any time soon.

Societal Pressures on Women and Girls

Noelle Howey

Pressure to have sex comes in many forms and from many sources. Many women have sex even when they're not emotionally ready for the experience. Noelle Howey, a freelance writer who writes about teen problems and women's issues, discusses some of the pressures women face to have sex. Many women have sex, she writes, because they want to feel desirable, because they want to seem sexually uninhibited, or because they do not want to come across as a tease.

Y ou would never describe Melissa,* 25, known for belting out raunchy drinking songs at office parties, as sexually timid. But she knew she didn't want to have sex on her first date with Ryan. "I wasn't up for it," she says. "I thought, 'Maybe we'll do it on the third or fourth date.'" So, at midnight, as she stood up to leave his apartment after chatting with him for a few hours, she was surprised when he blocked the door. "Don't go," he coaxed. "I don't want you to leave." Half an hour later, when

*Names have been changed to protect privacy.

she tried once more to go home, he grabbed her hand and asked her to stay. They had sex. Though she didn't object, Melissa was furious with him for being so insistent—and with herself for giving in.

Pressured and Manipulated

Chances are, Melissa's experience isn't that foreign to you. Almost all sexually active women have similar stories to tell—about times when they felt pressured, manipulated, intimidated or trapped into having intercourse, when they didn't say no but never said yes—but many of them maintain a self-defeating policy of silence about these episodes. Says Melissa, "I know it would have helped to confide in my friends, but I was so ashamed of myself for not doing anything more to stop him."

Anna, 28, shudders whenever she remembers her date with Doug five years ago. After they went out to dinner, they came back to his place and kissed for a while. She wasn't that attracted to him, but she enjoyed making out. He removed her shirt and bra. They kissed some more, then he excused himself. When he reentered the room, he was wearing nothing but an open terry-cloth bathrobe and was carrying a condom. "I was stunned," Anna says. "But since Doug acted like it was a given we'd have sex, I felt like I couldn't turn him down." Afterward, he smoked a cigarette. She spent a sleepless night lying next to him.

> Almost all sexually active women have . . . felt pressured, manipulated, intimidated or trapped into having intercourse, when they didn't say no but never said yes.

A few weeks later, she ran into him on the street. He asked in a flirtatious way, "Why haven't you called me?" She stammered something about being busy, and fled. She was livid, but she felt unjustified in being so angry, because, as she puts it, "It was my fault. If I hadn't fooled around with him, this wouldn't have happened. And it's not like he raped me or anything."

That's true. According to Carol Sanger, J.D., a professor at Columbia University Law School, rape is generally defined in most states as forcible sexual intercourse. But high-pressure sex—or sex obtained without regard for the woman's desire, through pressure, intimidation or intentional manipulation—seems to be much more common. According to the landmark 1995 Sex in America study conducted by researchers at the University of Chicago—astonishingly, the only recent major study to address this topic—more than one out of five women say they have been coerced into having sex. Feminist Naomi Wolf, author of *Promiscuities* (Fawcett Columbine, 1998), thinks the real numbers are higher: "It's absolutely universal. Every woman I've talked to about this has gone through it." Liz Grauerholz, Ph.D., associate professor of sociology at Purdue University and coeditor of the book *Sexual Coercion* (Lexington, 1991), agrees. "When I get together with groups of women, just about everybody has had this experience to different degrees," she says. "But women are hesitant to label it. Also, they don't want to seem like they're saying they've gone through something that's in any way the same as being a rape victim."

> [High-pressure sex] relies more heavily on manipulation and subtler forms of psychological warfare—pleading, presuming or wearing the other person down.

High-pressure sex shouldn't be confused with date rape, though the line between them is blurry. The difference lies in the use of force. Date rape often involves a degree of physical force, but it may also be marked by intense intimidation or some other overt form of psychological coercion, like social or emotional blackmail. Another crucial point: The woman expresses her lack of consent in an obvious way—either by trying to fend the man off, by saying, "No," "I don't want to" or "Please don't," or by expressing emotional distress or anger—and the date rapist overrides, ignores or pretends to misread her.

But, unlike date rape, which isn't consensual at all, high-pressure sex is ambiguous because it does involve some form of consent. It relies more heavily on manipulation and subtler forms of psychological warfare—pleading, presuming or wearing the other person down. While the date rapist actively inspires and exploits a woman's terror, the man in high-pressure sex plays on emotions like pity, guilt, insecurity, embarrassment or, in some cases, fear.

Why "No" Can Be Such a Difficult Word

Just saying "No" has never been as easy as it sounds. Many smart, independent women who can forcefully assert their opinion in a meeting or argue a point in a courtroom have found themselves relinquishing power in the bedroom. Why do we persist in going along?

• *We don't want to be a bad date.* Melissa, for instance, was interested in pursuing a relationship with Ryan: "I wasn't that attracted to him, but he seemed nice. I liked him." If a guy is insistent, we may think, "Oh, this is important to him, so I might as well." In a context of trust and equality, that might be okay. But without that trust—which can only be established over time—the woman who has sex before she's ready is likely to end up feeling used.

> The woman who has sex before she's ready is likely to end up feeling used.

"Women are taught to put men's needs above their own," points out Dr. Grauerholz. "By the time girls hit puberty, they can clearly see that men are more privileged, which reinforces the idea that men have a right to make these demands and to pressure them into having sex." Those lessons may come from home, where Mom has a job but still does all the housework, while Dad relaxes with the newspaper. Or they may come from school: Studies repeatedly show that teachers call on girls less frequently than on boys, and take their opinions less seriously.

Such everyday situations convey to girls that males possess more authority, so that by the time we're in the crucible of junior high and our self-esteem frequently plummets—we've already learned to muffle ourselves, to question our own judgment and to realize that to get along, it might be better to give in.

Female Bullies

Women aren't the only ones feeling pressured. Sixteen percent of men in a recent survey said they'd been blackmailed, guilt-tripped or otherwise psychologically coerced into intercourse, says Cindy Struckman-Johnson, Ph.D., professor of applied psychology at the University of South Dakota in Vermillion and coauthor of *Sexually Aggressive Women: Current Perspectives.* While male and female "bullies" have some similarities— they're highly aroused and driven by the prospect of dominating and controlling another person—there's a distinct difference in how victims from each gender cope. "Women who've been sexually intimidated tend to avoid sex and men in general," says Dr. Struckman-Johnson, while men who described themselves as "strongly affected" by a traumatic incident try to steer clear of particularly aggressive women but still retain the same openness toward women and relationships.

Noelle Howey, *Mademoiselle*, August 1998.

• *We don't want to come across as a "tease."* It's a common assumption that women only have a small window of time in which to speak up. "I'm already in his apartment," we might think. "Can I still say no? What about if I've kissed him? Let him touch my breasts? Or taken off my clothes?" Rationally, most women realize that they have the right to say no at any point up to—and even during—intercourse. But that doesn't always silence the nagging feeling that we can't say no after a certain point, because then, we fear, we'll be accused of leading him on.

When she was a teenager, Audrey would get to a point, somewhere between heavy petting and getting completely naked, when she felt she had to "follow through" whether she wanted to or not. "I took it for granted that you had to get guys off once it got to a certain point," Audrey, now 25, says, "So I ended up going down on a lot of guys or having sex with them because I thought I had to, that it was part of the bargain. My friends and I all assumed we had to."

> Rationally, most women realize that they have the right to say no at any point . . . but that doesn't always silence the nagging feeling that . . . we'll be accused of leading him on.

• *We want to seem sexually uninhibited and savvy.* Women are not only afraid of letting down their male partners; they're also afraid of disappointing themselves. Thanks to the sexual revolution, women feel they have the total and complete power to say . . . yes. But what if we don't want to, because we're not ready, we're not feeling well or simply aren't in the mood? Anna remembers wanting to say no, but she "didn't want to seem like this little girl."

"Some women think, 'Oh, I'm a hip, liberated chick. I can't say no,'" points out Wolf. "The ideal is this Ally McBeal-by-day, Debbie-Does-Dallas-by-night figure who always manages to deliver a high-quality sexual experience. Most young women don't want to be seen as backward." Ironically enough, the price we pay for living up to that sexy modern image may be our voice.

• *On the other hand, we're afraid of coming across as too sexually savvy.* Much of this confusion would be alleviated if women simply asked for what they *did* want in bed. Kate, who reluctantly ended up having sex with a blind date, would have been "perfectly happy doing a little petting, you know? He could have touched my breasts, but I didn't want to have sex." But as Wolf says, "Women aren't allowed to be clear about what they want. You're not supposed to say something like 'You can go down on me, but let's not have intercourse,' because our culture says not to talk about these things. Our culture says if you use those words, you're a slut."

Kate agrees. "There's no way I could have told him what I was okay with. I would have felt like I was trying to talk dirty. I would rather have had sex I didn't want than say anything to him." According to Wolf, this phenomenon is incredibly common. "You're not supposed to talk about anything," she says. "Instead, you're supposed to get swept away, like when people get drunk and hook up. That's supposed to be sexy."

• *We need to feel that men find us desirable.* Anna says, "I have a friend, Kim, who's successful and beautiful and intelligent, but she doesn't see any of these good points." Some women focus on male attention as the main measure of their self-worth and see a man's sexual interest—even if he's slick or pushy—as validation. "Kim met a cute guy at a party the other night, and she ended up having sex with him," recounts Anna. "She hadn't wanted to sleep with him, but she gave in because, she told me, 'I felt lucky that he noticed me.'"

Men Aren't Always the Villains

What makes high-pressure sex even harder to deal with is that in some cases, no one is to blame. The guy—far from being an assailant—is baffled about what his female partner wants, and honestly believes she's interested in having sex.

This isn't unusual, even among experienced men. "Some guys don't know how to recognize female desire," says Wolf. "Many can't tell whether a woman is sending out signals she doesn't want to go further." And some women assume that men can interpret their body language, and are irritated when they don't.

But there are also men who don't try to understand what's going on. They're the ones who've bought into an idea that still permeates popular culture: Women secretly long to be sexually dominated. These men might not actually assault their dates, but they rely on the implied passive threat of physical violence to get their way.

DON'T FALL

You WOULD IF You LOVED ME

EVERY ONE'S DOING IT!

I WON'T HURT YOU

FOR A LINE

From *Sex Respect*® by Colleen Kelly Mast, ©1997. Used with permission from Respect, Inc.

Suzanna, 24, had sex with Daniel on the third date—only because she wasn't sure he'd take no for an answer. After she had a drink with him at her apartment, he held her against the wall and kissed her. "Let's slow down," Suzanna whispered. "All he said was, 'Why? Don't you like me?' He had this smile on his face, a weird smile, like he didn't want to stop. All I could think was 'It's better if I just go along with him. I won't get hurt this way.'" Although she submitted to Daniel out of fear, Suzanna insists that he didn't rape her. "I could have told him to leave," she says. "I could have spoken up, at least. I definitely wasn't his victim. But he knew what he was doing; he knew he was freaking me out, and I think that excited him."

Dealing with the Aftermath

Coping with the consequences of high-pressure sex can be difficult. As Suzanna explains, "I felt pissed and angry and helpless. There was no way to get revenge."

Certainly not through the court system: These situations are *not* prosecutable. But, as Dr. Grauerholz asserts, "That doesn't mean it's moral and excusable." Unlike a rape victim, a woman who suffers after being manipulated into sex bears some responsibility for its occurrence. And that feeling of culpability keeps many women silent about what actually went on.

According to Andrea Parrot, Ph.D., associate professor of policy analysis at Cornell University and an acquaintance-rape expert, turning blame inward—common among victims of assault or rape—is endemic in high-pressure sex cases. "In so-called 'gray zone cases,'" says Dr. Parrot, "fewer people believe you have genuinely suffered as a result of the incident. You're less likely to tell others how you feel, including your friends. You're more likely to deal with it yourself, thinking it's all your fault because it's not a straightforward assault." This self-blame is harmful, says Dr. Grauerholz, because "pressured sex has negative emotional effects: lowered self-esteem, and the feeling that you're not in control of your sexuality. The idea that women are painting themselves as victims and need to quit whining can end up silencing them."

The social critic Camille Paglia has even suggested that coercive incidents should be considered a rite of passage, a consequence of being sexually active. Many women believe this, too, and dismiss high-pressure sex as "just bad dates." Audrey says, "It could be thought of as bad sex, as something everyone goes through." But these experiences are about being intimidated or manipulated into intercourse, and, frequently, they involve the implicit threat of assault to obtain consent. Such an abuse of male power should never be considered "normal" sex.

How to Get Your Own Way in Bed

Women need to realize they're entitled to say no, and they should practice saying it out loud. "Come up with five sentences that you can say to a date, like 'I don't want to do this' or 'I have to leave because I have to get up early for work,'" advises Madeline Breckinridge, A.C.S.W., clinical social worker and director of the Sexual Abuse Treatment and Training Institute in New York City. If you've had high-pressure sex in the past, you need to figure out why. "I wanted to impress Doug," notes Anna. "He was older and so much more experienced, and I was nervous about seeming unsophisticated." Revisit your "bad dates." Was it fear of rejection? Or disappointing yourself? Then, consider: Was caving in to that fear worth feeling crummy afterward? Realize that each time you "give in," you're chipping away at your belief in your right and power to speak up. "I kept beating myself up because I did nothing to stop him," says Anna. "It was only one incident, but it made me feel so weak and stupid."

Finally, we need to take these experiences seriously. Because as long as we keep quiet about high-pressure sex and its often painful consequences, it will go unrecognized. After all, before the term "date rape" was coined, few people believed it existed, and women were assigned responsibility for any "unpleasantness." "It would help if there were a word," says Dr. Grauerholz. "It would give us the language to help process our feelings." Call it "high-pressure sex," and talk about your experiences with your friends and male partners. Audrey agrees: "The awful times I had shouldn't be accepted as a part of life."

My Boyfriend Wants Sex

Liz

A fourteen-year-old girl writes that her boyfriend says she should have sex with him to prove that she loves him. She's not ready for sex yet, she says, despite the fact that he tells her all their friends are doing it. But, she's afraid he'll break up with her unless she gives in. Liz, an online teen counselor, tells her that if her boyfriend really cared about her, he wouldn't ask her to have sex when she's not ready.

C hris, 14, has a boyfriend, Rick, who wants to have sex with her. She doesn't think she wants to, but she's afraid she'll lose him.

Chris's Story

Rick keeps pushing me. I don't know if he's telling the truth—that they're all doing it . . . I mean, it's not exactly the kind of thing I can ask my friends in school, is it? Not even Dara. We're close, but not that close.

I don't really want to, but he keeps saying if I love him, I should prove it. I'm happy with the way things are now. It feels good just to fool around and touch each other, and I like the kissing. Not so much when he tries to put his tongue in my mouth,

Reprinted with permission from "How Far Should I Go: A Monologue in One Act," by WholeFamily Inc., available at www.wholefamily.com.

that's kind of pushy. But I feel safe just having him hold me. I even let him put his hands under my blouse. Why do we have to do more than that, anyway? And what about all that AIDS stuff, and getting pregnant? I wouldn't want a kid at my age! Rick says, "Don't worry, I'll take care of everything." But he's missing the point.

> He keeps saying if I love him, I should prove it.

I'm afraid if I don't go along with him, he'll drop me and find someone else. I really don't want that, but I don't like feeling pressured either. Anyhow, who says my next boyfriend won't ask for the same thing?

I wonder if April and Andy really did it. Rick says that Andy told him they do it all the time—whenever her parents are out and she baby-sits for her baby sister he comes over. But I can't imagine them. Maybe I can just ask her if it hurt the first time. . . I'm afraid of that too. It's easy for the boy—he's not the one it's gonna hurt.

I'm Not Ready Yet

Every time we're alone somewhere, Rick keeps asking me if I'm ready, or am I still chicken. He even showed me the condom he keeps in his wallet for when I'll say yes. I want to keep checking to see if he still has it or if he gave up on me and tried it with someone else, but I can't ask that! He says he really loves me, but it makes me think that if he loved me, he wouldn't ask me to do it, knowing how I feel about it.

The problem is. . . . I'm not so sure how I really feel.

I saw him looking at Laura. Maybe he'll ask her out if I don't say yes. I wish I could decide if I really want to do this—I don't feel ready yet. Once we start, he'll probably want it all the time.

Why can't we leave things the way they are right now? I just feel it's going too fast for me. Rick says it's not healthy for a guy to get so hot and then stop—but what about me? I get turned on, too, but nothing happens to me when we stop. It just takes a while to cool down and then I'm okay. Could he be right about guys, though? I wouldn't want to hurt him in any way, but I don't want to do it just for that reason.

It's not fair that he says I don't really love him if I won't say yes. I do love him . . . I think so, anyway.

It's too bad Mom's gone. I know I could have talked this over with her. I guess I'll just have to work it out for myself. I wish there was someone I could talk to.

Why can't we just leave things the way they are till we're older?

Chris, 14

Liz Tells It Like It Is

To all the "Chris's" out there saying "I wish there was someone I could talk to," you need to know that sometimes there isn't. In the real world, you may sometimes feel as if you're alone, which is too bad, since this topic may be the most difficult one you'll ever have to deal with in your teen years.

Hopefully, there will be parents or friends or school counselors who can help you out, but part of becoming an adult is acknowledging that the buck stops with you. And this is certainly the case when the issue is your sexual life.

So here's Liz, to tell it like it is. Chris, all Rick wants is to feel good for a while. He could care less about your mind, your emotions and your soul. Maybe some

> I'm afraid if I don't go along with him, he'll drop me and find someone else.

day he'll grow up and he will care about those things, but from your description of him, he's still far, far away from that point.

Because if he really cared about you as a person, he wouldn't just be trying to have sex with you. I know that's hard to hear. Everyone wants to feel wanted, for whatever reason. Maybe you haven't yet experienced the wonderful high you can feel when a guy wants to hang out with you because you're bright, or funny, or fun, and not just because he wants to have sex with you.

It would be great if you could find someone to talk to, but this is a topic that is difficult to discuss with anyone, even your closest girlfriends. And maybe the average teenage girl won't feel comfortable discussing this with a parent, relative or teacher.

But sometimes help comes from strange places, like a cool staff member at the school, an adult neighbor who you babysit for and—who knows—maybe you're one of those lucky kids who can talk to her parents. Hey, when I'm not doing this WholeFamily stuff, I'm a parent and teacher, and I'd sure like to believe that my kids or students could come to me.

> If he really cared about you as a person, he wouldn't just be trying to have sex with you.

As for friends—sometimes it's even hard for good friends to keep a secret. And you never know what's going on in the head of a friend. For instance, if you have a girlfriend who's doing it, but she's not so sure she's doing the right thing, it might make her feel better if she knows that you're doing it too.

But me, I'll keep your secret, because I don't know you from Eve anyway and I have no plans to contact your parents, so trust me—you're safe.

Which is maybe a poor choice of words—safe—since if there is one thing that teenage sex is not, it's "safe."

Teenage sex is not safe.

Teenage Sex Is Not Safe

And here are some of the reasons it's not safe:

1. Sex is a heavy responsibility, not just a feel-good sport. And the first responsibility you have is to yourself. For girls, more than for boys, it's something that involves your deepest feelings, your most intimate connection between your body and your soul, and it's not something that you should share lightly. I mean, who is this guy, anyway? Do you really feel like letting him deep into

your soul? Into your body? Just so you'll have someone to hang out with on Saturday nights?

2. You can get AIDS from sex (not to mention a lot of other diseases), and anyone who tells you that condoms are foolproof is a proven fool. Some doctors say condoms are only 80% foolproof (and if they are really 90% foolproof, or 95%—does that make you feel any better?).

3. You can get pregnant from sex. So there's good news and bad news:

4. If you didn't get pregnant, there's nothing to worry about (physically, maybe) and if you did, there's good news and bad news:

5. If your parents don't make you feel like a lowlife for the rest of your life for getting an abortion, then there's good news and bad news:

6. If the abortion goes okay, you'll be back on the market for the next cruising cat, but if it doesn't, then there's good news and bad news:

7. If you only get slightly messed up, you might still have a kid or two, but if not, then there's good news and bad news:

8. If you lose your ability to have children, you might not want children anyway, but if you do, then there's good news and bad news:

9. If there are still girls out there stupid enough to get pregnant, then you might consider adoption, but then there's good news and bad news:

10. If they're all having abortions like you, there'll be no babies left to adopt.

The Real Questions

The real questions that you may (or should) be asking yourself are:

How does this sex thing fit in with my values, my emotions,

my comfort or discomfort with myself sexually, my place (status?) among my friends—both girlfriends and male friends, my feelings about what my parents and other adults whom I respect would think about this, etc.

Each person is different so each person has different questions. Obviously, you have questions, or you wouldn't be reading this.

Chris, take it from me—if you want sex to be a special part of your life, save it to share with someone whom you want to make a special part of your life, too.

And I'm not talking about your high school life (unless you plan on settling down at the age of seventeen). Sure, you'll be missing out on a lot of superficial fun right now—maybe even on some stuff that isn't so superficial—but hang in there. If all we cared about was feeling good for the moment, we'd still be swinging from trees.

I know this doesn't sound cool and some of the guys will laugh at you, but when the right one comes along, he'll think that you're amazing.

But a question still remains: If you're not having sex with him and you feel that you don't really know why, and you feel a void in your life because of it, and you feel you should be filling that void with something, what are you going to fill it with?

That's a question that only you can answer.

Hang in there.

Keep in touch.

Fondly,

Liz

My Girlfriend Wants Sex

Lucie Walters

In this question-and-answer column, a teenage boy asks for help in resisting his girlfriend's pressure to have sex. Lucie Walters, whose syndicated advice column is published in newspapers in Louisiana, Alabama, and Florida, tells him that people who pressure their partners into having sex show no concern for their partners' feelings. Recent columns by Lucie Walters are available at www.lucie.com.

L ucie—I'm 15 and being pressured. I have an older girlfriend who wants to have sex. I want to, but don't know if I should.

I have to ask advice from a total stranger off the Net. Sad, huh? No offense. What should I do?

—Peace Out

Peace out—No offense taken. I am a stranger, but helping teens anonymously is my job. That probably fits for you right now because you seem to be looking for an objective opinion. If you read my bio online, you'll see that I have been doing this for many years.

Reprinted with permission from "Dear Lucie Says to Keep Your Morals and Ask Lots of Questions," *Adolessons* column from March 15, 2000, at www.lucie.com.

Who would you feel safe to ask? Your parents would be up-set, and probably try to end the relationship (which may be a safe way out for you). My guess is that most of your male friends would not be able to relate and may start teasing you. You realize that, so you found me.

A Life-Altering Decision

I don't know your girlfriend's age or where you live. Having sex with you could get her into legal trouble.

Unfortunately, many people consider your situation enviable. In fact, they wouldn't see a problem here. Some readers won't even believe your letter.

You seem like a moral guy struggling with deciding when and

The Effect of Peer Pressure on Teens

Peer pressure, "the most blamed" factor, . . . contributes to in-creased teen sexual activity. B. Herjanic states that young ado-lescents below the age of 15 were probably the most vulnerable to pressures to engage in sex, as well as to the consequences of pregnancy. In a survey of 625 teens . . . , 43 percent of boys aged 15–18, 65 percent of girls aged 15–16, and 48 percent of girls aged 17–18 answered affirmatively to the question, "Have there been times when you have been on a date, when you had sexu-al contact even though you really did not feel like it?" J. Billy and J. Udry's research showed that best male friends influence females' sexual activity, but they could not determine if the best friend was a sexual partner of the girls questioned. Despite the assumption that females become sexually active because they cannot say no to their boyfriends, research by G. Cvetkovich and B. Grote suggests that neither can some boys say no to their girlfriends.

La Wanda Ravoira and Andrew L. Cherry Jr., *Social Bonds and Teenage Pregnancy,* 1992.

---

with whom you should begin having sex. I don't know if the issue is simply whether or not to have sex with this girl. Could be the reason you're feeling so pressured is because this is a *life-altering decision,* and it encompasses a great deal more than this one situation.

You are right! Your life would never be the same again. Maybe you believe that sex means love and commitment, even marriage, and you don't want this relationship to become that involved. To many females, making love means making a commitment.

Being Pushed Feels Uncomfortable

Also, your girlfriend is pressuring you. Regardless of gender, being pushed feels uncomfortable. Can you trust her?

My suggestion is to decide (as objectively as you can) what is the appropriate time and situation for you to begin having sexual intercourse. Factor in your moral and religious beliefs. Include the dangers involved vs. the pleasures derived.

Decide in the cool of the day, not the heat of the night.

Until then, congratulate yourself on good boundaries and morals.

Chapter

Sex and Consequences

The Emotional Side of Sex

Shauna

Having sex is an act of physical and emotional intimacy. Despite all the hopes and plans you may have for your first time, you may not be prepared for the emotions you'll experience afterwards. In the following essay, Shauna describes how her expectations of a beautiful and romantic experience were shattered by the totally unexpected emotions she felt afterward. With the help of her understanding boyfriend, Shauna was able to work through her feelings, but she warns that some teens may not be prepared for the emotional intensity of sex until they are more mature. Shauna is a teen writer for TeenWire.com, an online teen magazine published by the Planned Parenthood Federation of America.

I didn't lose my virginity—I know exactly where I left it.

It was three days past my 18th birthday with my boyfriend, Curtis, who was also a virgin. We were in love—in crazy, desperate, earthshaking love, and we wanted our first time to be special.

Everything was perfect: He was a wonderful, caring, decent man. I knew I didn't have to worry about him running back to his buddies to brag about his "score." We were in my own bed, we used protection, we were "old enough," and we were relaxed and happy.

I remember the romantic way I had envisioned it happening—it would feel wonderful and I was supposed to feel wonderful afterwards—mature and fulfilled.

"The Big Lie"

I now refer to that idea as "The Big Lie."

I'm not saying it can't be that way, I'm just saying that soap operas and romance novels don't exactly paint an accurate picture of losing your virginity.

> "Soap operas and romance novels don't exactly paint an accurate picture of losing your virginity."

Here's the truth:

It's awkward.

It's confusing.

It can hurt.

And for most women, having an orgasm is very unlikely.

Worse yet, I was completely unprepared for how emotionally lost I would feel afterward.

Unexpected Feelings

Instead of feeling like I'd crossed some sacred threshold into true womanhood, I felt like I'd just slammed the door on ever being a little girl again. I was 18—an adult by legal standards—and yet there was still a little girl inside of me who wasn't quite ready to let go of who she was. I felt as if I'd given away a part of me that I could never get back.

I think I assumed too much. I thought that since my partner loved me a great deal and we'd given the event so much forethought, I would be left with a rosy "afterglow" instead of the emptiness I felt.

Simply because I was 18—older and more emotionally mature than many are when they lose their virginity—I was strong enough and resilient enough to get through it. My partner and I already had a strong relationship, so I talked to him about the feelings I was having. We worked through them together and had a loving relationship for two more years before we finally went our separate ways.

I don't think it would have been any easier for me if I'd waited longer, but I'm grateful that I waited as long as I did—and that I chose the right boy. It helped me to deal with the unexpected feelings that came up.

Although I think we'd all like sex to be spontaneous, I've learned that it requires a great deal of thought and planning—for adults and teens alike. And that involves several things: choosing a partner, making sure you have and use protection against pregnancy and infection, keeping realistic expectations of the experience, and waiting until you know that you can handle the feelings that may come up afterward.

In the end, I have no regrets about how or with whom it happened. But I always feel so sad for the girl or boy who has a first sexual experience too early and may be unable to cope with feelings that might have been much easier to handle later on.

Loss of Self-Respect

Fetima Perkins

It's said that girls and women often use sex to get love, meaning that they'll have sex with someone with the hope that a one-night stand will turn into a long-term relationship. What many don't realize, however, is that those who constantly search for "love" in this manner frequently lose their sense of self-esteem and self-respect. Fetima Perkins describes how her search for love led to her promiscuous behavior with guys who were just using her for sex, and her realization that she doesn't have to have sex with every guy she meets. Fetima Perkins writes for *New Youth Connections*, a New York City magazine by and for teens.

My boyfriend had always known about my past, but one day toward the beginning of our relationship, he asked me how many guys I'd had sex with.

"A lot," I said. But he wanted a specific number.

I was shocked when I counted and realized the answer was 21. That even shocked him.

So then I asked him the same question, and when he answered, I was speechless for the first time in my life.

He said, "One."

I don't think I ever felt so bad in my life. Not even when

Reprinted from "Looking for Love," by Fetima Perkins, *New Youth Connections,* January/February 1998. Reprinted with permission from Youth Communications.

people called me names did I ever feel that bad. When I came out of shock, I burst into tears.

Looking for Mr. Right

He told me I shouldn't be upset—I really am a nice girl who didn't know what she wanted from a man, he said.

Actually, I did know what I wanted from a man—the problem was, I didn't know how to get it.

I wanted someone who would give me all the love and support I didn't feel like I got at home. What I got instead was just sex.

I guess I figured that if I could find a nice guy to treat me right, he would automatically take the place of my father, who left home when I was in the sixth grade.

I was very hurt when my father left because we had such a good relationship. We would go to Florida by ourselves for the weekend and leave my mother home.

> I wanted someone who would give me all the love and support I didn't feel like I got at home. What I got instead was just sex.

We'd go out to dinner and to the movies. And it meant a lot to me that (and this may sound silly) we even had special names for each other.

If we had such a good relationship, why was he leaving me? What had I done wrong?

I Started to Rebel

After my father left, I was upset and depressed, and I began to rebel against my mother.

I felt like I couldn't really depend on her for the love I needed because she's not very open. She says I can talk to her, but I don't think I can.

I didn't know any other way to vent my feelings, so I would keep all my anger inside and wait until she got me upset. Then I'd go off on her.

I always wanted to tell her my problems and tell her what I was doing with my life, but it seems like the older I got, the harder it was for me to tell her anything. I feel like my life is one big secret.

After my dad left, I also shrugged off all my girl friends. They couldn't do anything for me except tell me where all the cute guys were going to be at. They couldn't help me with my real problems.

Feeling Empty Inside

I felt like I had no one to talk to and I didn't feel close to anyone anymore. Eventually I started to feel empty inside.

I only knew one way to fill that empty space, and that was to depend on a guy emotionally the way that I used to depend on my father.

I was 12½ years old when my father left, and by my 13th birthday, I had lost my virginity. I wasn't proud of it, but how could I change it, it was already gone.

The first time I had sex, it was the biggest surprise in my life that it happened.

At the time, I was mad at my boyfriend and wanted to get back at him. My other boyfriend took me to a friend's house and we had sex in his brother's room.

"The Most Naive Virgin in the World"

I had no intention of doing that. I went to our friend's house as the most naive virgin in the world, honestly thinking that nothing would happen if we were alone.

Later I found out we weren't even alone: There was one guy watching from under the bed and another guy watching from the next room.

Once it was all over and the audience was gone, I didn't even know how to feel. But I didn't feel bad until I found out that the guy under the bed wanted to know if he was next.

When I got home, I went into my room and wrote in my diary. That's when it really hit me. I thought to myself, "Fetima, you just had sex with someone who doesn't even love you!"

I sat there and cried.

To make things worse, that boyfriend broke up with me two days later.

I didn't have sex again for a while. I figured I wouldn't want to do it again. But when the urge did arise, I didn't fight it. I made out with all these guys who came my way, and my name was scattered all over my neighborhood.

I Thought They'd Love Me

I never really felt that I had to go all the way with these guys, but that's the way it happened.

I had this I-don't-care attitude, but I did care even though I wouldn't admit I did. I would cry every night thinking about what I was doing and how I felt. Still, I couldn't seem to change.

I always wondered to myself, "What the hell is your problem? Don't you know you could catch something and die?"

I never had an answer for any of the questions that I asked myself. I felt like a lost soul walking through a graveyard, trying to find someone to take care of me, but never picking the right one.

10 Times out of 10, I Was Wrong

I would always go into the bedroom thinking this guy might actually like me. Then when we finished and everyone knew about it the next day, I would realize I was wrong again.

But again and again my feelings would get intertwined way too much. I'd get a big knot in my chest and think it was love.

Then I would get upset with the guys when they didn't return my feelings, even though I knew deep down inside that they hardly even knew me. And the truth is that I really didn't know them either.

Like I met this one guy who didn't act like a typical guy. After we had sex, he didn't say, "Get out of my house." He let me sleep over and he made me lunch.

After that, I wanted to tell him, "I love you."

It's not so much that I thought that sex would lead to love, but I guess that as a girl, I thought everyone felt close after they had sex. Ten times out of 10, I ended up being the only one who felt something at the end of the night.

I guess I just had to learn the hard way that some guys will tell you anything to keep you in their houses a little while longer.

Called a "H-" and a "Sl-t"

Most people who found out what I was doing labeled me a h- and a sl-t. They never tried to find out what was wrong, and just assumed I was doing this for the fun of it.

But I never enjoyed myself. I mean, I enjoy having sex whether I like the sex or not but mostly because I enjoy pleasing the person I'm with.

> I would always go into the bedroom thinking this guy might actually like me. Then when we finished . . . I would realize I was wrong again.

I don't know why I feel I have to satisfy other people all the time. I don't want to hurt anyone's feelings and I'm afraid they might think less of me if I don't do what they want me to do.

I tend not to tell people what I truly feel. Even when I can't or just don't want to do what they ask, I usually just say what the person wants to hear.

For example, I was going out with this guy who didn't bother acting slick like the other guys. He made it clear he just wanted me for sex.

Hard to Say "No"

One day I didn't feel like being bothered, but I also didn't feel like I could tell him I didn't want to have sex. So while he was in the bathroom, I just took my stuff and left.

The next day I saw him driving as I was walking home from work. He stopped the car in the middle of the street and yelled, "That was really f—ked up what you did, you stupid b-tch!"

Being with that guy made me look at my other relationships. I said to myself, "Fetima, you're so stupid!"

If I'd had two other hands, I would have beat myself up.

Trying to Change

I never knew just how bad I felt about myself until a good male friend of mine wrote me a letter telling me it was high time I take a look in the mirror and saw that I was not the person I was being.

When I read his letter, I started to cry. I had never really thought I was a h- or a sl-t, because I always wanted to be something and stay in school. I thought that made me different.

I mean, some girls get caught up in guys so much, they don't even go to school. I didn't go to school at times because being with this one guy seemed more important.

But after a while I stopped letting guys interfere with my education. At least they couldn't call me a *stupid* sl-t.

My friend's letter made me see that I was acting like a sl-t, even though I knew I was worth more than that.

A Serious, Not Sexual, Relationship

The person who really helped me calm down is my boyfriend. He and I have been together for almost three years now, even though we've argued, cheated on each other and even broken up.

He has helped me realize who I am and who I want to be. I didn't have sex with him for a whole year, kind of as a test to see if he'd wait—and he did.

He wanted a serious, not just a sexual, relationship. That made me feel more confident in myself.

Now I can proudly say that while I haven't made a 180 degree turnaround in my life, I have made a 90. I'm really proud of myself for that. Some people can't even make a 9.

I Wish I Never Had Sex

These days, I am still flirty and I still feel like having sex with some guys I meet (and sometimes I do). But I'm working on being monogamous.

When I tell guys, "No," I feel proud of myself. To myself, I'm like, "You go, girl!"

I always tell younger girls that I wish I had never had sex in the first place. I know that if someone had told me that, like most teenagers I probably would have gone and tried it anyway.

> I was acting like a sl-t, even though I knew I was worth more than that.

But I think it's important for girls to know that having sex with every guy, or even a select few, isn't cool.

In my opinion, there is nothing wrong with having responsible sex, but if you don't want to have sex, or you don't enjoy having sex, you shouldn't do it.

Show a Girl You Care

Plus, sex is risky. Of course, you can get pregnant. And it's the '90s—there are millions of people out there with AIDS and other diseases. We teenagers think that it's never going to happen to us. (It does!)

And if you're the type to call a girl names and make her feel bad—well, take it from someone who has been there, it hurts like hell.

In the same time that it takes to call someone a slut or a whore, you could take some time out to talk to her. Ask her why she chooses to do the things that she does.

She may be surprised at first by your asking, but I bet she will be happy that you cared enough to ask.

Being Used for Sex

Rebecca Lanning

Teens who are going through a difficult time, such as a move to a new school, may feel like they don't fit in and sometimes have less confidence in themselves. In an attempt to overcome these feelings of loneliness and become popular, they may sometimes make decisions they'll later regret. In this essay, a lonely teenage girl finds that attention from a cute boy in her new school makes her feel better about herself. Because she's lost her self-confidence, she's easily persuaded to have sex with him when he tells her things she wants to hear about herself. When she discovers he was just using her for sex, she realizes that self-esteem must come from within, not from others. Rebecca Lanning is a writer for *'Teen* magazine.

If you didn't know her, you might think 16-year-old Brittany* had it all together. She's really cute, in a Meg Ryan kind of way, with swingy blond hair and a smile that can light up a room. You'd think she'd never had one moment of self-doubt. But she keeps a secret tucked inside of her, a secret of shame, sadness and loss. Here is her story.

*Names and identifying details have been changed.

Excepted from "He Only Wanted Me for Sex," by Rebecca Lanning, *'Teen,* August 1995. Reprinted with permission from *'Teen* magazine.

Brittany's Story

This is really hard for me to talk about. Whenever I think back on all that's happened, I feel these waves of grief. Like someone died or something. And I want to go back and try to fix it, change the whole story so that it has a different ending. But I can't do that. I used to pray that I'd wake up and be my old self again. But then I'd run into him somewhere. Or someone would mention his name. Or I'd just see a car like his, and I'd fall apart.

> I wish I could just take a giant eraser, and erase the whole thing from my life.

Sometimes, my eyes would tear up and I could squeeze them shut and swallow hard and kind of swallow the pain and be OK. But other times, I couldn't shut it off that easily. Like one day at school. I was sitting there in biology, and I saw him pass by in the hall. I saw him for, what, a millisecond? And I lost it. I had to be excused. I went to the girls' bathroom and closed myself up in a stall and leaned against the door and just cried. Total sobbing. Those giant, heaving sobs, like when you can't even catch your breath. I felt so stupid, but I couldn't get a grip. And then my face was all red and splotchy, and I looked like I'd been beaten up or something. And I guess I had been, in a way, beaten up from the inside. It's hard to make the hurt go away.

It's not like I even want to be with him again. I mean, I did for a while, but now I just want to put it all behind me. I want it all to be like ancient history. Or not even history. I want it to be like it never happened at all. I wish I could just take a giant eraser, and erase the whole thing from my life.

Trying to Connect

I think things started to unravel when my family moved. We built this house that was like a mile from our old house, and we moved at the end of my freshman year. When I was a freshman, I was really popular. I was on student council, and I was a junior varsity cheerleader and I had a great boyfriend named Hayes. He was really good to me. Even though he wanted us to have sex, he never pressured me. And at that time, having sex was the last thing on my mind. I never even considered it.

Then, during that summer, before my sophomore year, the school district changed, and that fall, I had to go to a different high school where I knew only about two people. Even though I tried to make friends and get involved in stuff at my new school, it just didn't come that easily for me. It was like everybody was already in their set groups. I couldn't find a niche, you know, where I felt accepted. I ate lunch by myself a lot. I was really lonely. I went to some club meetings, but nobody would really talk to me that much. I felt like I was invisible. I'd try to get together with some friends from my old school, but it's like I didn't really fit in with them anymore. I guess I didn't want them to know what a hard time I was having at my new school, so I didn't really reach out to them. Then Hayes and I started having problems because we didn't see each other as much. And when we were together, I was always so bummed out that he didn't know how to handle it. We broke up the last week in September. Over the next couple of weeks, I sort of gave up on myself. Then in October, I met Tad.

I had never felt that kind of attraction before in my life! He had wavy, brown hair and brown, sort-of-flirty eyes and these shoulders that went on for miles. He played soccer, so he was really in shape. I could just look at him and melt. He had Spanish right before I did, and I always passed him coming out of the

He tried to get me to go further, but I wouldn't. He said I wasn't any fun. I wanted him to think I was fun so that he'd want to be with me.

room where the class was. At first, we just smiled at each other. And then one day he said, "hi," and pretty soon we were meeting between classes and talking. Every morning when I woke up, I thought about when I would see Tad and that gave me energy, you know, to get up and get going. All morning, I'd think about stuff I could say to him. And then after we'd talked, I'd feel pumped up and that would help me get through the day.

One day when we were talking, he invited me to eat lunch with him. I thought it was just going to be us, but he showed up with two of his friends, Ward and Peter. They were juniors like him; they were on the soccer team too, and we walked over to this deli. They were pretty wild, kind of loud and acting crazy. I remember, Tad pulled me on his lap. I was kind of nervous, but at the same time I was really happy. It felt so good to be close to him and to be eating lunch with him. I soaked up the attention. I ended up paying for everybody's lunch.

After that, I ate lunch with Tad, Ward and Peter every day. I wouldn't say much. But I'd smile a lot and laugh at their jokes. Sometimes, they'd ask me personal stuff. Looking back, I realize that these guys were jerks. But at the time, I thought I was privileged to hang out with them.

Crossing the Line

One night, I went out with Tad and Peter and Ward. We drove around and went to a couple of parties. Later, after they dropped me off, Tad threw rocks at my bedroom window, and then he climbed up the rain gutter, onto the roof and into my room. My parents weren't there; they were at the symphony, but I didn't tell Tad that. We talked quietly, and then he turned off the light and stood close to me. I let him kiss me and unbutton the top of my nightgown. He tried to get me to go further, but I wouldn't. He said I wasn't any fun. I wanted him to think I was fun so that he'd want to be with me.

> I think I felt that having sex . . . was going to make everything better.

The next weekend, I went out with Tad and his friends again. This time, they got some beer and we went out to this field near the airport.

The next thing I knew, Tad had grabbed a sleeping bag and he was leading me by the hand away from the Jeep and into the woods. He was being sort of funny about it, sort of dancing with me. He had a couple of beers with him, and he was trying to get me to drink one, but I wouldn't. Then he spread the sleeping bag out, and he pulled me down next to him. He started telling me how beautiful I was, how much he liked me. The next thing I knew, he was on top of me. He was saying all these wonderful things to me, like how right it was for us to be together. He

> I think maybe he liked the challenge of trying to get me to have sex more than he liked actually having sex.

was being really gentle, really sweet. It felt so good to be close to him, but at that point I still wasn't going to give in. But then he said I was beautiful. And that made me feel so happy. I started feeling my old confidence coming back, and it's so ironic because that's when I started giving in. I think I felt that having sex with Tad was going to make everything better. I'd just been doubting myself so much, and here was this guy who didn't have any doubts about me. I think I wanted to be accepted so bad, I wanted to feel like I belonged somewhere again, and so we had sex.

Holding On

The next few days were kind of weird. Those bad feelings about myself hadn't gone away. If anything, I felt worse. I couldn't make sense of it all. Tad was still nice to me, but it's like something had shifted between us. He didn't look at me the same way. Maybe it was my imagination, but it seemed like he didn't look at me at all.

My interest in him grew. Even though I was beginning to make some friends at school, I started feeling really dependent on Tad. He hadn't promised me anything. I'd just assumed that we'd be together because we'd had sex. But, obviously, he didn't feel the same way. I couldn't believe that Tad could've said all those things to me and then tossed me aside. Was it just a big act so he could get me to have sex with him?

I think maybe he was surprised that I had given in to him, even though that's what he wanted. I think maybe he liked the challenge of trying to get me to have sex more than he liked actually having sex. And I guess I wasn't much of a challenge anyway, so he sort of lost interest.

> Being self-assured, feeling good about who I am, has to come from the inside.

I became really clingy, calling him up all the time and crying if he couldn't meet me somewhere or see me. I constantly tried to figure out where he was.

We ended up having sex again, twice. Both times I was the one who initiated it. One time was at Peter's house after school. The other time was at my house, in my room. I really regret that time especially because whenever I look at my bed that's what I think about. That will never go away.

I thought having sex would make things better, but it didn't. After I lost my virginity, I guess I felt like I didn't have anything else to offer.

Looking Back

My friend finally talked me into seeing a school counselor. That's when I knew things were out of control. The counselor helped me put together the pieces of what had happened. She helped me deal with all the stuff that I was feeling.

It's been over a year now, and things are better. I can actually have a conversation with Tad and not break down. I don't even blame him so much for what happened anymore. I just feel sad. He smooth-talked me into doing something I wasn't ready for. I was at a very vulnerable place, and I was looking to him to make it all better. He took something from me that I'll never be able to get back. But I also learned something. That being self-assured, feeling good about who I am, has to come from the inside. Nobody can make me feel secure but me.

I'm on the gymnastics team now, and I was elected to the homecoming court and the National Honor Society. That meant a lot to me, but I'm still not completely over what happened. I have a hard time dating guys because I think that they know I'm not a virgin and that's why they're interested in me. There's this little voice inside of me that keeps trying to convince me that I'm OK. That I'm still a good person. But when I look in the mirror, it's not always her voice I hear. Sometimes it's a nagging, critical voice.

I wish I could go back in time and change what happened. I'd go back to the first day at my new school. I'd try harder to make friends and not expect to fit in overnight. I'd reach out more. I'd be more honest about how hard all the changes were for me instead of pretending that everything was OK.

I'd like to go back to that night in the woods with the planes going overhead. I wouldn't have gone anywhere near that sleeping bag. What I'd really like to do is to go back to that first night I let Tad come in my room. I wouldn't have let things go so far.

A Ruined Relationship

Mari Kinney

There are many different reasons why teens decide to have sex. Mari Kinney writes about a friend of hers who had sex with her boyfriend in an attempt to save her relationship. She found out sex doesn't always act as glue; her boyfriend soon dropped her anyway for someone else. Kinney was sixteen years old in 1996 when this essay was written.

Everyone who is anyone seems to be having sex. I'm not saying that every single person is having sex, but having sex is just as common as smoking weed. Pretty much everyone has tried it at least once.

It's too scary out there for me. Even safe sex doesn't seem that safe. But I think the thing that scares me most about sex is how much it hurts when your relationship doesn't work out. This happened to my friend and it broke my heart—hers too, I guess.

When Lovers Break Up

When I was 12, I hooked up two friends of mine. I knew they would be a great couple. They were both sweet and thoughtful and had great personalities. At school everyone envied them. They were always holding hands, totally lovey-dovey. He got her rings and bracelets for her birthday. One time at school he

Reprinted from "Teen Sex: Too Scary Out There for Me," by Mari Kinney, *LA Youth*, December 7, 1996. Reprinted with permission from *LA Youth*.

hired some guys to come and sing her favorite song, "Always and Forever," then later took her and her family out to the Red Lobster. She once got him an autographed Cowboys jersey, his favorite team.

He'd carry her books for her, and one Christmas, gave her all his hard-earned Christmas money so she could visit her family in Guatemala for the holidays.

> The more she wouldn't put out, the more aggravated and distant he got.

But two years later, things took a turn for the worse. The spark was fading. They didn't go out much. The couple that everyone had once envied seemed just like any other couple. He wanted to do more than just make out. To be honest, so did she, but her family was Catholic. Her mom always said, "Your virginity is everything. Don't ever give it away. Only to the man that you marry and love."

The more she wouldn't put out, the more aggravated and distant he got. It was, "Sorry, I forgot about the date." "I forgot about your birthday." "I forgot to call you back—I was busy." They were breaking up and getting back together every other day.

Fighting to Save a Relationship

One day she told me she had the solution—to have sex. She said, "This will make everything better." I said, "No, this is what he wants." I tried to convince both of them it was just going to make everything worse. But they were like, tonight's the night. They shut me out. She was fighting to save a relationship that wasn't meant to be.

The next day they were all happy, holding hands again. Then two weeks later, she came to me. "What am I going to do? My period hasn't come."

She called me the next day. She was pregnant. She had to tell her boyfriend and her parents.

She invited me over to be there when she told him. His response was: "Are you sure it's mine?" She gave away her treasure to this guy, and he was basically saying she was a tramp.

The next day, he wanted to know why she didn't get an abortion. She told him she could never do that because it was against the teachings of the Catholic church. Meanwhile, her parents were upset. They wanted to know how she was going to take care of a baby.

She was a smart, college-bound girl with good grades. So they looked into adoption. I think this was the right decision, because she couldn't excel in school and take care of a baby.

The months went by. Everybody at school could tell she was pregnant. But her relationship with her boyfriend got worse. He wouldn't take her calls, he wasn't there. When my friend was six months pregnant, he wanted to see other people. She reminded him that it was his kid, too. He said, I'm too young to be taking care of a kid. So she was on her own.

In her seventh month she stayed home because of complications. She had her baby in her eighth month and gave it away for adoption. I haven't seen her since then because her parents sent her away to Guatemala so she could learn some values.

Sex Messed Everything Up

So in the end, they split up and I lost both their friendships. Sex messed everything up. I think teens should think about the love and friendship they are putting at risk when they have sex, not to mention the risk of pregnancy and AIDS. These days, the only person you can trust is yourself. That's why I have better things to do than go out there and lose my virginity.

> We all feel lonely and want to feel loved, but sex won't fix that.

I think we all feel lonely and want to feel loved, but sex won't fix that. It's just a temporary physical act. I don't know exactly how you find love, but I know you can't fix things instantly by having sex.

Pregnancy

Marshall Brain

The following article by Marshall Brain, author of *The Teenager's Guide to the Real World*, gives sexually active girls the facts about their chances of becoming pregnant. No contraception, except abstinence, is 100 percent effective against pregnancy, so pregnancy can result even if a couple uses protection. The purpose of sex is to create a baby, writes Brain, so a couple should not have sex unless they are prepared to make the commitment—both financial and personal—to raise a child for the rest of their lives.

Should you pursue or have sex as a teenager? This is an option, and you get to make the decision. Like any other decision, however, there are things you should keep in mind. Here are three of the more important:

- Fact #1: If two people have unprotected sex long enough, they will get pregnant.
- Fact #2: This comes from the October 1996 issue of *Scientific American* magazine: "Six out of 10 women having abortions used protection." What that says is two people who have protected sex have a pretty good chance of pregnancy as well.
- Fact #3: If two people have sex and one of them is carrying a sexually transmitted disease, then the other person has

Reprinted from "Teenage Sex Is an Option," by Marshall Brain, *The Teenager's Guide to the Real World*. Reprinted with permission from BYG Publishing.

some probability of getting the disease, even when the couple uses protection.

Think of these three facts as "disadvantages." They tend to be good reasons not to have sex as a teenager. None of them have ever stopped anyone from having sex, however. You can look at the rate of infection for STDs, the number of abortions performed every year and the number of unwed teenage mothers to see that.

> If two people have unprotected sex long enough, they will get pregnant.

To any adult the three disadvantages make it "obvious" that teenagers should not have sex. What adults generally forget is that for many teens the brain and body are sending signals that indicate otherwise. The question for you as a teenager is, "Should logic win this one?" Your body has a desire to reproduce. To your body sex is important. Can you discipline yourself enough to live with the urges and wait until you get married? That is the question.

The Purpose of Sex Is to Make a Baby

Here are two things to keep in mind as you are making that decision:

- By having sex, you are making a hidden commitment to the child that results. The purpose of sex is to create a baby. Therefore, by having sex you are saying, "I am willing to care for the baby."
- Babies carry with them a lot of baggage. They need constant attention, they cost a lot and they require two people. Therefore, once you and your friend create a baby you will need to get married, and then the two of you will need to care for the child for the next 20 years. That means you will give up a tremendous amount of personal and financial freedom. Spend some time with someone who has a baby and see how much work is involved before you underestimate the amount of care a baby requires.

If you decide to have pre-marital sex, do it with the understanding that once a child is conceived, you are responsible for the care and well-being of your mate and the child for the next 20 years. The hospital bill alone for a normal childbirth is $5,000 to $10,000. Do you have that money? If not, then why would you have sex? Never mind the cost of housing, feeding, clothing your spouse and the child.

Facts About Teen Pregnancy

How widespread is teen pregnancy in the U.S.?

More than 4 out of 10 young women become pregnant at least once before they reach the age of 20. Nearly one million teen girls become pregnant every year, (that's 12% of all teen girls who have had sexual intercourse.)

Don't a lot of teens want to get pregnant?

No. The overwhelming majority—78 percent—of pregnancies to 15–19 year old teen girls are not planned. Among younger teens, 15–17 year olds, 83 percent of pregnancies are unplanned. In addition, most . . . sexually active teens today use contraception.

What's the future for teen parents and their babies?

• Only 1/3 of teenage mothers receive a high school diploma.

• Nearly 80 percent of unmarried teen mothers end up on welfare.

• The children of teenage mothers have lower birth weights, are more likely to perform poorly in school, and are at greater risk of abuse and neglect.

• The sons of teen mothers are 13% more likely to end up in prison. The daughters of teen mothers are 22% more likely to become teen mothers themselves.

National Campaign to Prevent Teen Pregnancy, *Facts and Figures*, no date.

The correct path is to find someone you are madly in love with and want to spend the rest of your life with, then decide that the two of you want to have a child, then get married, then save up enough money to provide a stable environment for a baby and then conceive a baby. Have a baby within a strong marriage that is ready to support the child: It is best for the baby and best for the parents.

> Once a child is conceived, you are responsible for the care and well-being of your mate and the child for the next 20 years.

As an unmarried teenager there is one other fact that you should keep in mind. You generally don't hear much about this fact, but it is important. You are doing your thing right now. You are meeting people, going out, having fun. That is all fine. You have this vague notion in your head that one day you will get married. That is also fine. But eventually you will find someone who you want to marry, and it will become much less vague. You are going to be deeply in love with this person. You are going to be with this person for the rest of your life. That is a fact.

On the night of your wedding you are going to be with that person in bed. There are two options on that first night you are together. Either it will be the first time for you, and therefore it is going to be special. Or it will not. If both of you are able to come to bed and learn about sex with each other and share that throughout your lives, it is a good thing. It is an incredible gift to give to someone. Maybe your partner cannot give it to you. That is OK. You can still give it to him or her.

A Long-Term Commitment

In general, teenage sex is like drugs. It seems like it should feel good when you do it, but longer term it often feels bad. It is a "cheap thrill" that has little or no value. It also tries to separate sex from babies, which is impossible. Keep in mind that the purpose of sex is to create a baby, and that a baby is an incredible long-term commitment. You should not be attempting to create a baby unless you are willing to make that commitment. If you want to make that commitment, you should be getting married first for the sake of the baby. That is a fact of life.

Abortion

Liz

For women, discovering that you're pregnant when you don't want to be gives new meaning to the word "panic." Liz, an advice columnist for an online teen advice website, *www.wholefamily.com*, writes about her decision to have an abortion when she was a teenager. Although her abortion went smoothly, her relationship with her boyfriend was never the same, and the experience was one she'll never forget.

You're late. At first you figure it's just nerves. After all, you took precautions. I mean, you were always careful, except maybe that one time.

So you buy one of those home pregnancy tests. You sneak it into the house and spend one crazy, long night reading the instructions over and over again. The next morning, your entire being becomes fixated upon that unmistakable, red POSITIVE circle sitting at the bottom of a plastic tube.

Panic

For the first time in your life, you understand the full meaning of the word "panic." Your heart drops into a deep, dark place you had no idea existed in your body, but you know it's not moving until you get yourself out of this mess.

The crazy thing is that while your world is falling apart, some

Reprinted with permission from "Liz on Teen Pregnancy," by WholeFamily Inc., available at www.wholefamily.com.

neighbor down the street took that same test and also got a positive. Only she's running down the hall to tell her husband the good news. But life's sort of funny that way.

Okay girls, Liz knows how you're feeling—believe me, 'cause I've been there. Now, we're not going to talk about Pro Life vs. Pro Choice—this is not about that. This is about taking control of a difficult situation by surrounding yourself with the people who love and care about you the most and getting some good, solid guidance.

> For the first time in your life, you understand the full meaning of the word "panic."

Your first step may be to contact a school counselor or empathetic teacher. You'll probably need someone to help you approach your parents. Now you're thinking, "Liz, there's no way I can tell my parents." As rough as this may seem, believe me, it can be done. . . .

Liz's Story

But now I'd like to share something with you. Liz has her own story to tell. Several years ago I was staring at my positive result at the bottom of a cup. If only I had known then what I know now, but Liz was just too full of herself to ask for assistance from the right people. I decided to do things my way.

Back then, I figured that "Pro Life" meant no life left for me and whoever coined the phrase "Pro Choice" had a sick sense of humor. I mean wasn't it my need to be free and make my own choices that got me into this mess? Believe me, there was nothing free about being a pregnant teen. And feeling that there was no way out other than abortion wasn't much of a choice.

I couldn't bear the secret alone, so I told my best friend and of course, I also told him, after all, he was the father. But I guess this news was just too hot for them to handle, 'cause by the time I got to school, all eyes were upon me (or maybe it was just my imagination).

My trusted "friend" volunteered to contact the local abortion clinics. Meanwhile the other "responsible" party figured he could raise at least most of the cash. After all, he was the father.

As the days went by, the panic and fear only became worse. I couldn't sleep. I looked like hell and my body sort of floated through space, like I was no longer grounded and I didn't know where I was headed. And I kept saying over and over to myself, "What have I done? What have I done?"

Then my day at the clinic arrived. He came with me and so did my "friend," who had by now told the whole continent.

Facts About Abortion

- Nearly 4 in 10 teen pregnancies (excluding those ending in miscarriages) are terminated by abortion. There were about 274,000 abortions among teens in 1996.

- Since 1980, abortion rates among sexually experienced teens have declined steadily, because fewer teens are becoming pregnant, and in recent years, fewer pregnant teens have chosen to have an abortion.

- The reasons most often given by teens for choosing to have an abortion are being concerned about how having a baby would change their lives, feeling that they are not mature enough to have a child and having financial problems.

- 29 states currently have mandatory parental involvement laws in effect for a minor seeking an abortion: AL, AR, DE, GA, ID, IN, IO, KS, KY, LA, MD, MA, MI, MN, MS, MO, NE, NC, ND, OH, PA, RI, SC, SD, UT, VA, WV, WI and WY.

- 61% of minors who have abortions do so with at least one parent's knowledge; 45% of parents are told by their daughter. The great majority of parents support their daughter's decision to have an abortion.

Alan Guttmacher Institute, *Facts in Brief: Teen Sex and Pregnancy,* 1999.

The counselors were nice enough. They calmly informed me of the procedure and risks. They answered questions and for one selfless minute I thought to ask, "will the baby—er . . . fetus, embryo or whatever—feel pain?" But that fleeting thought was overtaken by fears for myself and instead I asked, "Will this hurt a lot?"

Things Were Never the Same Again

A few hours later, I lay at home no longer pregnant and the relief that I thought I'd feel took the form of reflective depression mixed with anxiety, 'cause I had to keep hiding all bathroom evidence from my mother.

Aside from a phone call, I didn't hear from him much. But that's okay, 'cause I didn't want to repeat this episode again. But believe it or not, two weeks down the road when I was feeling lonely, hurt and vulnerable, he showed up at the door. You see, he had that urge and I was fair game once again. But things were never the same between us.

Hey, don't get me wrong, it's not like I didn't survive all of this. It's just that, well . . . take it from me, Liz—there are some things in life that you never forget.

Sexually Transmitted Diseases

Angie Maximo

Contracting a sexually transmitted disease is a real risk for teens, as they make up nearly 25 percent of all new cases of STDs. Angie Maximo discusses some of the most common sexually transmitted diseases—how they are contracted, what their symptoms are, and how (and if) they can be cured. Abstinence or condoms are the best defense against most STDs. Maximo is a writer for *Seventeen*.

N eed a good reason not to lose your virginity? How about six? Here's the deal on the most common sexually transmitted diseases (STDs).

Gonorrhea (aka the clap)

What is it? A supercontagious disease. Left untreated, it can cause pelvic inflammatory disease, stomach pain, bleeding between periods and infertility (translation: You can't have kids—ever). Women are less likely to notice symptoms than men.

How do you get it? Sexual intercourse or oral sex.

How do you know you have it? You have a greenish-yellow discharge and pelvic pain; you feel like you have to pee all the time, and it burns when you do. It usually takes about 10 days

Reprinted from "Sex Files: The Deal on STDs," by Angie Maximo, *Seventeen*, March 1997. Reprinted with permission from Primedia Publications.

for these symptoms to show up, but 80 percent of women who have it don't even get symptoms (that's why it's *so* important to visit a gynecologist if you're sexually active).

How do you get rid of it? Antibiotics. Many people with gonorrhea also have chlamydia and must be treated for both.

Your best defense? Condoms or abstinence.

Herpes (simplex virus 1 and 2)

What is it? A virus that causes painful blisters and sores on the genitals, mouth or other areas of the body.

How do you get it? Although the cold sores and blisters you get on your mouth are usually caused by herpes simplex 1, both kinds of herpes can be sexually transmitted. That means you can get it through touching, kissing, oral sex or intercourse.

> [Gonorrhea is] a supercontagious disease. Left untreated, it can cause pelvic inflammatory disease, stomach pain, bleeding between periods, and infertility.

How do you know you have it? Most people get blisters and open sores (ouch!) within two to 20 days after infection. But—warning—it can take *years* before you have that first breakout (um, surprise!). Other symptoms include itching and burning, fever and feeling run-down.

How do you get rid of it? Sorry—you can't. A drug called acyclovir can clear up the yucky sores and blisters, but the actual virus stays in your body forever. That means you can get breakouts again, and again, and again. . . .

Your best defense? Condoms or abstinence.

HPV (Human Papilloma Virus)

What is it? There are 60 different HPVs—some of which cause genital warts. HPV is often linked to cervical cancer.

How do you get it? Sexual intercourse or oral sex. Here's the tricky part: You can get HPV *even if* you use condoms. Because they don't cover all areas that might be infected.

How do you know you have it? Warts will usually pop up about two to three weeks after infection. They look like, well, warts. Some even resemble little cauliflowers. But this is another sneaky STD—you can have it and experience no symptoms. Or you can have the virus and not have a breakout until years later. The virus can also show up on a Pap smear, which you can have done by your gynecologist.

STD Stat

There are 12 million new cases of STDs every year, three million of them among teens.

One in four sexually active teens gets an STD by age 21.

The earlier you start having sex, the greater your chance of getting an STD.

Anyone can get an STD, whether the person has had one or 100 partners and showers twice a day or twice a week. No one has an I HAVE AN STD stamped on the forehead, so don't assume anything.

Teenagers are at greater risk of getting STDs because their immune systems are still developing.

Using condoms (rubbers, raincoats, love gloves—whatever) during sex can help protect you from STDs. But your best defense? Don't have sex—or wait until you've found a partner (someone you love would be ideal) who will get tested and be honest with you about his sexual history.

Angie Maximo, *Seventeen*, March 1997.

How do you get rid of it? The actual warts can be removed with special medicine (and we don't mean Compound W; this medicine must be prescribed by your gynecologist), laser surgery (zapping them with a laser beam) or cryosurgery (freezing them with liquid nitrogen). But, like herpes, this virus stays in your body forever.

Your best defense? Condoms (but again, condoms don't cover all areas that might be infected) or abstinence.

HIV (Human Immunodeficiency Virus)

What is it? This infection weakens the body's ability to fight disease and can cause AIDS (Acquired Immune Deficiency Syndrome). In the U.S., it's *the* leading cause of death for American women and men between the ages of 25 to 44.

How do you get it? The virus is in blood, semen, vaginal fluids and breast milk. That means you can get it through intercourse, oral sex, sharing contaminated needles or blood transfusions. Infected women can pass it to their babies while pregnant and in childbirth. You *can't,* however, get it from kissing, touching or from toilet seats. Keep in mind that HIV can live in the body for years before it causes symptoms, so you *can't* tell whether your partner is infected just by looking at him.

> HIV can live in the body for years before it causes symptoms, so you *can't* tell whether your partner is infected just by looking at him.

How do you know you have it? AIDS can cause rapid weight loss, diarrhea, flulike symptoms, thrush (a thick white coating on the tongue), major yeast infections and purple growths on the skin called lesions. Again, you could be infected with HIV and not show any symptoms for years.

How do you get rid of it? New treatments are giving AIDS patients hope, but so far there's no cure.

Your best defense? Condoms or abstinence.

Pubic Lice (aka crabs)

What is it? Critters that latch on to pubic and underarm hair, eyelashes and eyebrows. These little guys really do look like mini crabs (they're pale gray but get darker when they're swollen with blood).

How do you get it? Mostly through sexual contact (including petting), but you can also pick them up from infected sheets and clothes.

How do you know you have it? You'll know. Symptoms include intense itching (and we're not talking mosquito-bite itchy) of the genitals, a mild fever, irritability and fatigue, not to mention the freak-out factor of *seeing* the tiny critters on your body.

How do you get rid of it? Over-the-counter medicines like A-200 and Rid (the same stuff used to treat head lice).

Your best defense? You can't really protect yourself from crabs, so your best defense is abstinence.

Chlamydia

What is it? A bacterial infection that happens to be the most common STD—about four million cases a year in the U.S.! In women it can cause bladder infections, pelvic inflammatory disease and possibly even infertility.

How do you get it? Sexual intercourse.

How do you know you have it? This one's tricky. Most women have zero symptoms. But if it hurts to have sex (not just the first time but every time), if you have a weird discharge (read: anything that seems different from your usual discharge) or if it burns when you pee, you might have a case. As for your partner? Possible symptoms for him include penile discharge, burning and/or frequent urination and pain or swelling in his testicles.

How do you get rid of it? Take antibiotics prescribed by your doc.

Your best defense? Condoms or abstinence.

HIV and AIDS

Michelle Towner, as told to Stephanie Booth

AIDS is a sexually transmitted disease caused by the human immunodeficiency virus. The virus weakens your immune system to the point that it can no longer fight off infections, cancer, and other diseases. People can be infected with HIV and not even know it since it can take a decade or more before they start to show symptoms of the disease. In the following story, a teenage girl discovers that her longtime boyfriend unknowingly infected her with HIV. She's afraid to let her friends know her secret. Stephanie Booth is a freelance writer who writes about teen issues. Michelle Towner is the pseudonym of a teenage girl who contracted HIV.

I was 15 when I decided to have sex with Ben,* my first serious boyfriend. I worried that I'd get pregnant, not that I'd end up HIV positive. But that's exactly what happened.

I met Ben at the movie theater when I was 14. We ran in different circles because he was three years older than I was, but we liked a lot of the same music and movies and were both big Chicago Bulls fans. Ben was cute and sweet, and things between us got serious fast. When Ben brought up the idea of sex a few

---

* All names have been changed.

Reprinted from "I'm HIV Positive," by Michelle Towner, as told to Stephanie Booth, *Teen*, October 1999. Reprinted with permission from Stephanie Booth.

months later, it seemed right to me. We were in love.

We used a condom only about half the time we had sex. I knew you could get STDs that way, but Ben told me not to worry, and I trusted him. I knew he was more experienced than I was, so I figured he knew what he was talking about. The thought of HIV never crossed my mind—I would never have suggested we get tested before we had sex.

We dated for a year and a half, until I moved away. My father died when I was younger, and my mom and I never got along that great. So I decided to go live in a different section of Chicago with my aunt, who I was very close to. I knew that would mean Ben and I wouldn't see each other as much, and I worried that we'd drift apart.

Soon after the move, we did break up. I was crushed. I went back to my old neighborhood a couple of times, hoping to bump into him, but no one had seen him. I figured he had a new girlfriend, which made me feel even worse.

A Bad Diagnosis

About six months after I moved, I got really sick. I was running a high fever and throwing up, and I didn't have the energy to crawl out of bed for two days. My aunt made an appointment for me at the doctor, but she had to work, so I went by myself.

> I worried that I'd get pregnant, not that I'd end up HIV positive.

While the doctor examined me, he asked one question after another: "Do you drink?" "Do you do drugs?" "Do you smoke?" The answers were all no, until he asked if I'd had unprotected sex. "Just with my boyfriend," I said. He asked if he could test me for HIV, and I was like, "Why not?" I was sure I didn't have it. They took some blood and said to call in a few days for the results. I blew it off because I still felt so sick and just wasn't in the mood.

The nurse wound up calling me and asked me to come back

in as soon as possible. I just thought, or hoped, they were going to give me different antibiotics. The HIV test was still in the back of my mind, though. Then I knew something was wrong when the nurse made me wait in the doctor's private office. By the time the doctor came in, my hands were all clammy and I was shaking. Then he dropped the bomb: "Michelle, you're HIV positive," he said.

My first thought was, "I'm dying." I felt so angry and confused. Then I asked myself, "How did this happen?" "Who gave this to

---

HIV and AIDS

- As of December 1998, 688,200 Americans had been reported with AIDS, and 410,800 of them had died, since the beginning of the epidemic in 1981. In 1997, an estimated 270,841 persons were living with AIDS. This represented a 12 percent increase in people living with AIDS from 1996 and was due, in large part, to new drug therapies that have improved survival rates and decreased the number of deaths among people with AIDS. Despite this decrease, AIDS remains a leading cause of death in most age groups—in 1997 it was the fifth leading cause of death in the 25–44 age group, the seventh leading cause of death in those aged 15–24, and the ninth leading cause of death in those aged 5–14.

- The greatest proportion of AIDS cases in the U.S. has always been among people in the 25–44 age group. In 1996, nearly 75 percent of Americans diagnosed with AIDS were in this group.

- While there has been a declining trend in the number of AIDS diagnoses, the number of HIV diagnoses has remained relatively stable. Estimates suggest that 650,000 to 900,000 Americans are now living with HIV, and at least 40,000 new HIV infections occur each year.

Planned Parenthood Federation of America, *Fact Sheet: Sexually Transmitted Infections*, October 1999.

---

me?" I didn't want to think it was Ben, but I hadn't had sex with anyone else. The doctor asked if there was anyone he could call for me, but I didn't want to tell my aunt. I was too ashamed.

The next week I faked being sick and hid in my bedroom. I worried that everyone at school would suddenly be able to tell I was HIV positive and wouldn't want to come near me, and I was scared that I would accidentally infect someone. Every time my aunt tried to talk to me, I screamed at her to leave me alone. The doctor gave me brochures about HIV, but I was too depressed to read them. I didn't feel like eating or sleeping. I just felt so alone. Then one night, I finally snuck the phone into my room and called an AIDS hotline that was on one of the brochures.

Return to the Living

I felt weird calling, but it was the best thing I could have done. The woman I spoke to that night was so understanding; she didn't preach to me. She referred me to an AIDS clinic, and I went the next day. Neal, a social worker there, gave me a shoulder to cry on. He told me lots of people with positive status live pretty normal lives for a long time, but I had to face up to being sick.

> I asked myself, . . . "Who gave this to me?" I didn't want to think it was [my boyfriend], but I hadn't had sex with anyone else.

The next time I met with Neal, I brought my aunt. She knew I was seeing someone for depression but didn't know the details. When Neal told her I was HIV positive, my aunt didn't believe it. She demanded I take a second blood test. When that came back positive, she hugged me for what felt like forever. "You have to take care of yourself," she said. My aunt's been so supportive. She helped me break the news to the rest of my family, and she tells them how I'm doing when I don't feel like talking about it.

The doctor gave me medicine, AZT, to take at exact times twice a day. At first it made me tired, and I got monster headaches and stomachaches. The side effects aren't as bad now, but I get sick really easily. I caught my aunt's cold and was in bed for days. Another time, I got dehydrated and was in the hospital for more than a week. A lot of people with HIV lose weight or get bad rashes, and every day I wake up scared to look in the mirror and see those symptoms. I go to the doctor every three months, and each time, I dread bad news—that I have full-blown AIDS. I'm OK so far, but I'll be on AZT for who knows how long.

Everything Has Changed

I'm trying to keep everything normal, but it feels like everything has changed. Eventually I'm going to have to tell my friends. Keeping this secret is so hard. But what do I say, "Hey, great outfit, and by the way, I'm positive"? I still hide my pills if they come over. Or if we're out and I have to take one, I make an excuse and run to the bathroom. Sleepovers are impossible. I think my friends would understand, but I don't want them to feel sorry for me or think I'm contagious and be scared off.

It's the same with any guy I date. I had a boyfriend, but I didn't let it get too intense. I'm not ready to go there. I kinda push guys away right now. Of course, if I found the right guy, I definitely would tell him before things got serious.

Looking back, I think Ben slept with a lot more girls than he told me about. I guess we should have talked more about sexual history and practised safe sex all the time. I'll never know whether or not he knew he was HIV positive. He's moved away, and I've moved on. I'm 17 now and training to be a peer counselor so I can talk to other kids about HIV. At least I have a chance to warn others. Each day I'm alive gives me another opportunity to get the word out.

Bibliography

Books

Eleanor Ayer   *It's OK to Say No: Choosing Sexual Abstinence.* New York: Rosen, 1997.

Brent A. Barlow   *Worth Waiting For: Sexual Abstinence Before Marriage.* Salt Lake City, UT: Deseret, 1995.

Nathalie Bartle and Susan Lieberman   *Venus in Blue Jeans: Why Mothers and Daughters Need to Talk About Sex.* Boston: Houghton Mifflin, 1998.

Michael J. Basso   *The Underground Guide to Teenage Sexuality: An Essential Handbook for Today's Teen and Parents.* Minneapolis, MN: Fairview Press, 1997.

Ruth Bell   *Changing Bodies, Changing Lives: A Book for Teens on Sex and Relationships.* New York: Times Books, 1998.

Karen Bouris   *The First Time: What Parents and Teenage Girls Should Know About "Losing Your Virginity."* Berkeley, CA: Conari Press, 1995.

Marshall Brain   *The Teenager's Guide to the Real World.* Raleigh, NC: BYG Publishing, 1997.

Jack Canfield, Mark Victor Hansen, and Kimberly Kirberger
Chicken Soup for the Teenage Soul: 101 Stories of Life, Love, and Learning. Deerfield Beach, FL: Health Communications, 1997.

Julie Endersbe
Teen Sex: Risks and Consequences. Mankato, MN: LifeMatters/Capstone Press, 2000.

E. James Lieberman and Karen Lieberman Troccoli
Like It Is: A Teen Sex Guide. Jefferson, NC: McFarland, 1998.

Beth McNeill and Bonnie Benson
Teen Sexuality: Responsible Decisions. Waco, TX: Health Edco, 1995.

Susan Browning Pogány
SexSmart: 501 Reasons to Hold Off on Sex. Minneapolis, MN: Fairview Press, 1998.

Michael A. Sommers and Annie Leah Sommers
Everything You Need to Know About Losing Your Virginity. New York: Rosen, 2000.

Joe White
Pure Excitement: A Radical Righteous Approach to Sex, Love and Dating. Colorado Springs, CO: Focus on the Family Publishing, 1996.

Periodicals

Rebecca Barry
"Are You Ready for Sex?" *Seventeen*, January 1996.

Bob Bartlett
"Intimacy 101 for Teens," *U.S. Catholic*, August 1999.

Elizabeth Benedict   "Please Touch Me," *Esquire*, September 1997.

Keith Blanchard   "From Here to Virginity," *Sassy*, September 1996.

Jane E. Brody   "Teenagers and Sex: Younger and More at Risk," *New York Times*, September 15, 1998.

Beth Dawes   "I Had an Abortion," *'Teen*, February 1997.

Kristina DeKoszmovsky   "From Here to Virginity," *Men's Health*, November 1996.

Francesca Delbanco   "The Spin on Teen Sex," *Seventeen*, September 1998.

Kathy Dobie   "The Only Girl in the Car," *Harper's*, August 1996.

Katherine Dowling   "Condoms Won't Keep Our Teens Safe," *U.S. Catholic*, January 1995.

Jill Eisenstadt   "The Virgin Bride," *New York Times Magazine*, June 16, 1996.

Nina Elder   "Teenagers and Herpes," *Better Homes and Gardens*, October 1999.

Thomas R. Eng   "The Hidden Epidemic," *Issues in Science and Technology*, Summer 1997.

Charlotte Faltermayer   "Listening in on Boy Talk," *Time*, June 15, 1998.

Sandy Fertman   "I Had a Sexually Transmitted Disease,"
                       'Teen, November 1997.

Gayle Forman   "Sex? No Thanks!" Seventeen, August
                       1999.

Valerie Frankel   "Almost Sex," Mademoiselle, October
                       1996.

Christine Gorman   "Teen Girls Beware," Time, August 24,
                       1998.

Susan Hayes   "AIDS in America," Scholastic Update,
                       October 20, 1997.

Sarah E. Hinlicky   "Subversive Virginity," First Things,
                       October 1998.

Amy M. Holmes   "Hook-Up U," National Review,
                       September 13, 1999.

Thomas Lickona   "Ten Consequences of Premature
                       Sexual Involvement," U.S. Catholic,
                       April 1996.

David Lipsky   "Sex on Campus," Rolling Stone, March
                       23, 1995.

————   "To Be Young and Gay," Rolling Stone,
                       August 6, 1998.

Linda Liu   "If You Have Sex, Read This . . . ,"
                       Mademoiselle, February 1999.

Lance Loud   "Sex, HIV, and You: Three Girls Living
                       with HIV Speak Out," Sassy, December
                       1996.

Hara Estroff Marano   "Sexual Issues Fan Parents' Fears," *New York Times*, July 2, 1997.

Angie Maximo   "Sex Files: The Deal on STDs," *Seventeen*, March 1997.

Celia Milne   "Sex and the Single Teen," *Maclean's*, December 28, 1998/ January 4, 1999.

Marianne R. Neifert   "Why Teen Sex Is Riskier than Ever," *McCall's*, August 1995.

Anne Novitt-Moreno   "Our Battle Against AIDS," *Current Health*, February 1996.

Stephen Rae   "Party of One," *Men's Health*, September 1995.

Billy Rayman   "Losin' It! Hey, Guys Are Virgins, Too . . . ," *Sassy*, August 1995.

Katie Roiphe   "The End of Innocence," *Vogue*, January 1998.

Rex Roberts   "AIDS: The New Generation," *Scholastic Update*, October 20, 1997.

Robert Rorke   "Coming Out in America," *Seventeen*, April 1999.

Jeannie I. Rosoff   "Helping Teenagers Avoid Negative Consequences of Sexual Activity," *USA Today*, May 1996.

Nancy Jo Sales   "The Sex Trap," *New York*, September 29, 1997.

Roger Scruton   "Very Safe Sex," *National Review*, July
                       28, 1997.

Michael Segell   "The Sex Men Lie About," *Esquire*,
                       September 1996.

Wendy Shalit   "Daughters of the (Sexual) Revolution,"
                       Commentary, December 1997.

Shaynee Snider   "STDs: Don't Be a Statistic," *'Teen*,
                       December 1999.

Leora Tanenbaum   "I Was a Teenage 'Slut'," *Ms.*
                       November/December 1996.

Sadie Van Gelder   "It's Who I Am," *Seventeen*, November
                       1996.

Peter Vilbig   "Life, Death, Sex," *Scholastic Update*,
                       October 20, 1997.

Paul C. Vitz   "Cupid's Broken Arrow," *Phi Delta
                       Kappan*, March 1999.

Catherine Walsh   "Catholic Singles and Sex," *America*,
                       February 11, 1995.

Julie Weingarden   "The High Price of Popularity," *'Teen*,
                       June 1999.

Naomi Wolf   "The Making of a Slut," *Ms.*, March/
                       April 1997.

Organizations and Websites

The editors have compiled the following list of organizations concerned with the issues debated in this book. The descriptions are derived from materials provided by the organizations. All have publications or information available for interested readers. The list was compiled on the date of publication of the present volume; the information provided here may change. Be aware that many organizations take several weeks or longer to respond to inquiries, so allow as much time as possible.

Advocates for Youth
1025 Vermont Ave. NW, Ste. 200, Washington, DC 20005
(202) 347-5700 • fax: (202) 347-2263
e-mail: info@advocatesforyouth.org
website: www.advocatesforyouth.org

Advocates for Youth is the only national organization focusing solely on pregnancy and HIV prevention among young people. It provides information, education, and advocacy to youth-serving agencies and professionals, policy makers, and the media. Among the organization's numerous publications are the brochures *Advice from Teens on Buying Condoms* and *Spread the Word—Not the Virus* and the pamphlet *How to Prevent Date Rape: Teen Tips*.

Alan Guttmacher Institute
120 Wall St., New York, NY 10005
(212) 248-1111 • fax: (212) 248-1951
e-mail: info@agi-usa.org • website: www.agi-usa.org

The institute works to protect and expand the reproductive choices of all women and men. It strives to ensure that people have access to the information and services they need to exercise their rights and responsibilities concerning sexual activity, reproduction, and family planning. Among the institute's publications are the books *Teenage Pregnancy in Industrialized Countries* and *Today's Adolescents, Tomorrow's Parents: A Portrait of the Americas* and the report "Sex and America's Teenagers."

American Civil Liberties Union (ACLU)
125 Broad St., 18th Fl., New York, NY 10004
(212) 549-2500 • fax: (212) 549-2646
website: www.aclu.org

The ACLU is a national organization that works to defend Americans' civil rights as guaranteed by the U.S. Constitution. It supports confidential reproductive health care for teens and civil rights for homosexuals. ACLU publications include the monthly *Civil Liberties Alert*, the quarterly newsletter *Civil Liberties*, the briefing paper "Reproductive Freedom: The Rights of Minors," as well as handbooks and pamphlets.

Child Trends, Inc. (CT)
4301 Connecticut Ave. NW, Ste. 100, Washington, DC 20008
(202) 362-5580 • fax: (202) 362-5533
e-mail: swilliams@childtrends.org
website: www.childtrends.org

CT works to provide accurate statistical and research information regarding children and their families in the United States and to educate the American public on the ways existing social trends, such as the increasing rate of teenage pregnancy, affect children. In addition to the annual newsletter *Facts at a Glance*, which presents the latest data on teen pregnancy rates for every state, CT also publishes the papers "Next-Steps and Best Bets:

Approaches to Preventing Adolescent Childbearing" and "Welfare and Adolescent Sex: The Effects of Family History, Benefit Levels, and Community Context."

Coalition for Positive Sexuality (CPS)
3712 N. Broadway, PMB #191, Chicago, IL 60613
(773) 604-1654
website: www.positive.org

The Coalition for Positive Sexuality is a grassroots direct-action group formed in the spring of 1992 by high school students and activists. CPS works to counteract the institutionalized misogyny, heterosexism, homophobia, racism, and ageism that students experience every day at school. It is dedicated to offering teens sexuality and safe sex education that is pro-woman, pro-lesbian/gay/ bisexual, pro-safe sex, and pro-choice. CPS publishes the pamphlet *Just Say Yes*.

Family Research Council (FRC)
801 G St. NW, Washington, DC 20001
(202) 393-2100 • fax: (202) 393-2134
e-mail: corrdept@frc.org • website: www.frc.org

The council is a research, resource, and education organization that promotes the traditional family, which the council defines as a group of people bound by marriage, blood, or adoption. It opposes schools' tolerance of homosexuality and condom distribution programs in schools. It also believes that pornography breaks up marriages and contributes to sexual violence. Among the council's numerous publications are the papers "Revolt of the Virgins," "Abstinence: The New Sexual Revolution," and "Abstinence Programs Show Promise in Reducing Sexual Activity and Pregnancy Among Teens."

Family Resource Coalition of America (FRCA)
20 N. Wacker Dr., Ste. 1100, Chicago, IL 60606
(312) 338-0900 • fax: (312) 338-1522
website: www.frca.org

FRCA is a national consulting and advocacy organization that seeks to strengthen and empower families and communities so they can foster the optimal development of children, teenagers, and adult family members. FRCA publishes the bimonthly newsletter *Connection*, the report "Family Involvement in Adolescent Pregnancy and Parenting Programs," and the fact sheet "Family Support Programs and Teen Parents."

Focus on the Family
Colorado Springs, CO 80995
(719) 531-5181 • fax: (719) 531-3424
website: www.fotf.org

Focus on the Family is an organization that promotes Christian values and strong family ties and that campaigns against pornography and homosexual rights laws. It publishes the monthly magazine *Focus on the Family* and the books *Love Won Out: A Remarkable Journey Out of Homosexuality* and *No Apologies . . . The Truth About Life, Love, and Sex.*

The Heritage Foundation
214 Massachusetts Ave. NE, Washington, DC 20002-4999
(202) 546-4400 • fax: (202) 546-8328
e-mail: info@heritage.org • website: www.heritage.org

The Heritage Foundation is a public policy research institute that supports the ideas of limited government and the free-market system. It promotes the view that the welfare system has contributed to the problems of illegitimacy and teenage pregnancy. Among the foundation's numerous publications is its Backgrounder series, which includes "Liberal Welfare Programs: What the Data Show on Programs for Teenage Mothers," the paper "Rising Illegitimacy: America's Social Catastrophe," and the bulletin "How Congress Can Protect the Rights of Parents to Raise Their Children."

National Campaign to Prevent Teen Pregnancy
21 M St. NW, Ste. 300, Washington, DC 20037
(202) 261-5655
website: www.teenpregnancy.org

The mission of the National Campaign is to reduce teenage pregnancy by promoting values and activities that are consistent with a pregnancy-free adolescence. The campaign's goal is to reduce the pregnancy rate among teenage girls by one-third by the year 2005. The campaign publishes pamphlets, brochures, and opinion polls that include *No Easy Answers: Research Finding on Programs to Reduce Teen Pregnancy*, *Not Just for Girls: Involving Boys and Men in Teen Pregnancy Prevention*, and *Public Opinion Polls and Teen Pregnancy*.

National Organization on Adolescent Pregnancy, Parenting, and Prevention (NOAPPP)
2401 Pennsylvania Ave., Ste. 350, Washington, DC 20037
(202) 293-8370
e-mail: noappp@noappp.org • website: www.noappp.org

NOAPPP promotes comprehensive and coordinated services designed for the prevention and resolution of problems associated with adolescent pregnancy and parenthood. It supports families in setting standards that encourage the healthy development of children through loving, stable, relationships. NOAPPP publishes the quarterly *NOAPPP Network Newsletter* and various fact sheets on teen pregnancy.

Planned Parenthood Federation of America (PPFA)
810 Seventh Ave., New York, NY 10019
(212) 541-7800 • (212) 245-1845
e-mail: communications@ppfa.org
website: www.plannedparenthood.org

Planned Parenthood believes individuals have the right to control their own fertility without governmental interference. It promotes comprehensive sex education and provides contraceptive counseling and services through clinics across the United States. Its publications include the brochures *Guide to Birth Control: Seven Accepted Methods of Contraception*, *Teen Sex? It's Okay to Say No Way*, and the bimonthly newsletter *LinkLine*.

Project Reality
PO Box 97, Golf, IL 60029-0097
(847) 729-3298
e-mail: preality@pair.com
website: www.project-reality.pair.com

Project Reality has developed a sex education curriculum for junior and senior high students called Sex Respect. The program is designed to provide teenagers with information and to encourage sexual abstinence.

Sex Information and Education Council of Canada (SIECCAN)
850 Coxwell Ave., Toronto, ON M4C 5R1 Canada
(416) 466-5304 • fax: (416) 778-0785
e-mail: sieccan@web.net • website: www.sieccan.org

SIECCAN conducts research on sexual health and sexuality education. It publishes the *Canadian Journal of Human Sexuality* and the resource document *Common Questions About Sexual Health Education*, and maintains an information service for health professionals.

Sexuality Information and Education Council of the United States (SIECUS)

130 W. 42nd St., Ste. 350, New York, NY 10036-7802
(212) 819-9770 • fax: (212) 819-9776
e-mail: siecus@siecus.org • website: www.siecus.org

SIECUS is an organization of educators, physicians, social workers, and others who support the individual's right to acquire knowledge of sexuality and who encourage responsible sexual behavior. The council promotes comprehensive sex education for all children that includes AIDS education, teaching about homosexuality, and instruction about contraceptives and sexually transmitted diseases. Its publications include fact sheets, annotated bibliographies by topic, the booklet *Talk About Sex*, and the monthly *SIECUS Report*.

Teen-Aid

723 E. Jackson Ave., Spokane, WA 99207
(509) 482-2868 • fax: (509) 482-7994
e-mail: teenaid@teen-aid.org • website: www.teen-aid.org

Teen-Aid is an international organization that promotes traditional family values and sexual morality. It publishes a public school sex education curriculum, *Sexuality, Commitment and Family*, stressing sexual abstinence before marriage.

Websites

All About Sex

www.allaboutsex.org

This organization encourages teens to feel good about their sexuality. It believes that everyone—regardless of their marital status or sexual orientation—should enjoy and participate in sex. The website offers articles on virginity, sexual intercourse, masturbation, and sexual orientation, among other topics.

Dear Lucie

www.lucie.com

Lucie Walters writes a syndicated newspaper and online advice column for teens called Adolessons. Her columns discuss incest, sex, sexually transmitted diseases, pregnancy, love and relationships, and health. Visitors to the site can read archives of her columns as well as participate in message boards and chat rooms.

Teen Advice Online

www.teenadviceonline.org

TAO's teen counselors from around the world offer advice for teens on relationships and dating, sex and sexuality, gender issues, internet relationships, health, family, school, and substance abuse. Teens can submit questions to the counselors or read about similar problems in the archives.

Teenwire

www.teenwire.org

This website was created by Planned Parenthood to provide teens with information about sexuality and sexual health issues. The site offers an online teen magazine, searchable archives, a question-and-answer forum, and informative articles about teen issues.

Whole Family

www.wholefamily.com

This source is designed for both parents and teens. The site's advice columnist, Liz, answers questions about pregnancy, teen sex, drugs, drinking, and body image, while online articles discuss other issues such as divorce, relationships, and health.

Index